The
Knowledge

The
Knowledge

Your Football Questions Answered

Edited by
James Dart

guardianbooks

R23338
Waterstones
06/09

First published in 2008 by Guardian Books
119 Farringdon Road, London EC1R 3ER
guardianbooks.co.uk

A CIP catalogue record for this book is available
from the British Library.

ISBN: 978-0-85265-108-7

2 4 6 8 10 9 7 5 3 1

Designed and set by www.carrstudio.co.uk
Illustrations by www.jamielenman.com
Printed in Great Britain by CPI UK

Introduction

For the last eight years, readers of our weekly Knowledge football column have fired their questions, quibbles and general ramblings in our general direction and we've nerdishly scoured books, archives, websites and have even employed the odd bit of old-fashioned journalism in search of answers, solutions and truths behind the myths. "Who was manager of Norwich when they released Dion Dublin?" asked the snappily-monikered 100069602 in our very first edition on March 29 2000. Dave Stringer produced the relatively straightforward answer and the questions (and answers from our helpful readership around the world) have been flooding in ever since.

An irreverent and quirky tone akin to that of the Guardian's Notes and Queries page was soon set enabling those who read the column at guardian.co.uk/football every Wednesday to find answers to footballing questions that haven't been asked and answered a billion times before. Did Les Ferdinand MBE trash the Blue Peter garden? Is it true that an entire team were killed by lightning? Are Liverpool the worst performing European champions ever? In an age when football often pales into a bland impersonation of its former self, the Knowledge cares enough to ask these questions and provide the answers. The dedication of our writers and readers has enabled us to keep bringing you the interesting and offbeat facts and stories that you rarely find reported elsewhere on the football pages.

What follows is a collection of our favourite questions from guardian.co.uk readers and the answers faithfully provided by guardian.co.uk's football-writing team since the column's inception. From the time Norwich employed a flamethrower to thaw out their frozen pitch, to the awful albums released by footballers (including Kevin Keegan's Head Over Heels In Love (Move On Down)), this book brings together some of the weird, wonderful and often downright ludicrous facts about the game.

Ultimately, we are indebted to our readers who have contacted us from around the world to pose questions, contribute answers and have made the column what it is today. If you have a cunning or inane question to ask about the world of football, send it to our crack team of sleuths and assorted hacks at knowledge@guardian.co.uk. In the meantime we hope you'll enjoy the selections brought to you here.

James Dart

"Can you clear up whether this is truth or a myth: did a referee in Brazil actually shoot dead a player who disputed a penalty?"

It seems that Brazilian football's reputation has caused the odd Chinese whisper here: as far as we can tell, it is indeed a myth. But that hasn't stopped two referees in South Africa using guns to kill on the field of play. On February 20 1999, in Hartbeesfontein (around 125 miles south-west of Johannesburg), referee Lebogang Petrus Mokgethi, 34, shot and killed a player during a match between Hartbeesfontein Wallabies and Try Agains. According to police, when Try Agains scored to cut the Wallabies' lead to 2-1, Hartbeesfontein fans ran on to the field to protest (the game was believed to have been the subject of heavy unlicensed betting).

Amid the commotion, the Wallabies' 20-year-old captain Isaac Mkhwetha left the field to get a knife, while Mokgethi grabbed his licensed 9mm pistol from a friend in the crowd. According to witnesses, Mkhwetha lunged at Mokgethi with the knife, who responded by shooting the player in the chest. Mkhwetha died shortly afterwards. Mokgethi was released on bail after a court appearance where he pleaded not guilty to causing Mkhwetha's death. "It's easy for players and referees to get hurt during games in this area," shrugged the Wallabies' manager Isaac Mahlapsi.

Even more recently – in July 2004 – another official reacted, well, rather badly to criticism, as this Guardian account recalls: "A yellow card awarded to a player during a match between two local teams in Kenton-on-Sea in Eastern Cape province prompted protests from the coach and team. The coach of Marcelle club was hit in the chest and died on the pitch and two players were hit in their hands by the same bullet, according to the South African Press Association. "'There was an altercation and the referee became threatened when the other team approached him because they were angry,' said Inspector Mali Govender of Grahamstown police. 'So he pulled out a gun and killed the coach of the visiting team.' The referee fled the scene but police were confident he would be soon caught." The suspect in question was later named as Ncedisile Zakhe, described by the Kenton Soccer Association president Mziwanele Wopa as "one of my top four referees. I was shocked to see him do this."

"With Robbie Williams being invited to train with Bayern Munich, I was wondering which celebrities had trials with football clubs when they were younger?"

It's always been a bit peculiar to associate the majority of celebrities with significant football ability – like imagining your teachers in flagrante – but a number were on the books of league clubs, or at least had trials with them, in their youth.

Take chef Gordon Ramsay for a start: he played twice for Rangers' first team, against St Johnstone and Morton. "Both away and both shit in the sense that I played 20 minutes and 10 minutes," he reminisced in Observer Sport Monthly. "Of course it's so competitive that when I made it into the squad of 18 I wet myself with excitement, I was over the moon. But I was also very, very nervous. The games were really violent, not like the football we see nowadays. And then I got my bad injury. I tore my ligaments, and it was a heartache. I worked my way back to fitness but Jock Wallace was the Rangers manager then, and he was a Scottish version of Mike Tyson. When he wanted to rip your arse out, he would crucify you. I still remember him telling me they were letting me go. He was fucking ruthless. We were only in there about five minutes and I wanted to cry but I couldn't cry because I wouldn't even dream of crying anywhere near Jock Wallace. Then again I suppose I wouldn't be where I am today had they not been so ruthless. Because soon after I went on a catering course ..."

Perma-tanned crooner Julio Iglesias was also on the junior books of Real Madrid as a goalkeeper of some promise before a car crash in 1963 ended his career. Pope John Paul II was a keeper with hometown Polish team Wadowice, while Rod Stewart served an apprenticeship at Brentford before working out he could sing. "He trained with us for a week or two," recalled the Bees' deputy president Eric White, "and he may even have kicked a ball around with the juniors, but there is no record of Rod Stewart ever having signed to Brentford. Unfortunately, nobody at the club remembers his time here."

Samantha Fox briefly played for Arsenal's all-conquering female counterparts as a 14-year-old tomboy, before going on to Page Three stardom a couple of years later. "I love boxing, martial arts, and I used to play football for the Arsenal Ladies," she revealed. Former All Saints singer Shaznay Lewis also used to play for the Gunners, which came in handy when she took an acting role as captain of the Hounslow Harriers in the film Bend It Like Beckham.

Other celebrities who ultimately didn't quite make the grade include:

David Essex (Leyton Orient)
The Duke of Westminster (Fulham)
Sir David Frost (Nottingham Forest)

Anthony LaPaglia (Adelaide City/West Adelaide/Sydney FC owner – "I'm like a complete drug addict when it comes to football")

Ronnie O'Sullivan (Tottenham)

Gavin Rossdale (Chelsea)

Daley Thompson (Mansfield – "I was a clumsy centre-half. It was fantastic")

Jimmy Tarbuck (Brighton)

Stan Boardman (Liverpool)

Johnny Marr (Manchester City – "I was good enough for City, but they didn't follow up because I was probably the only player out there wearing eyeliner")

Mark Owen (Manchester United)

Bradley Walsh (Barnet/Watford/Brentford)

Ricky Tomlinson (Scunthorpe United)

Audley Harrison (Watford)

Angus Deayton (Crystal Palace)

Craig Charles (Tranmere)

Martin Kemp (Arsenal)

Nicky Byrne (Leeds)

Charlie Williams (Doncaster – actually, Williams made the grade with 171 appearances at centre-half: "[I was] never a fancy player, but could stop the buggers that were")

And then there are those who opted out of the footballing dream altogether. Sean Connery turned down trials, first with East Fife, and then with Manchester United, to become James Bond. "I really wanted to accept

[United] because I'd always loved the game," he said. "But I stopped to assess it and asked myself: what's the length of a footballer's career? It turned out to be one of my more intelligent moves."

"What is the largest number of game-ending injuries to have occurred to a single team during a match?"

The tragic case of Bena Tshadi in the Democratic Republic of Congo apparently holds this unfortunate record after a freak blast of lightning wiped them out mid-game. Back in October 1998, Bena Tshadi were drawing 1-1 with visitors Basangana in the eastern province of Kasai when a true bolt from the blue struck. "Lightning killed at a stroke 11 young people aged between 20 and 35 years during a football match," reported the daily newspaper L'Avenir in Kinshasa. The account added that while 30 other people received burns, "the athletes from Basangana curiously came out of this catastrophe unscathed." Immediately, accusations of witchcraft arose. "The exact nature of the lightning has divided the population in this region which is known for its use of fetishes in football," added the report. However, there has never been any official confirmation of L'Avenir's claims as much of the area was stricken by civil war.

This isn't the sole instance of lightning striking a football match, however. Just days before the Bena Tshadi incident, a South African Premier League game between Moroko Swallows and Jomo Cosmos was abandoned after seven players from both teams and the referee were sent sprawling to the turf. Three Swallows players – Jaconia Cibi, Peter Matitse and Benjamin Njemo – were knocked unconscious, but all thankfully recovered. Cibi later paid tribute to "God and my ancestors for saving my life . . . I do not even want to entertain the idea that it could have been a muti-related act."

"Is it really true that a Romanian side once built a moat filled with crocodiles to stop the crowd from invading the pitch?"

Incredibly, this snappy piece of hooligan deterrence actually was planned. Back in 2003, Fourth Division side Steaua Nicolae Balcescu found themselves in a quandary: Romanian league chiefs were threatening the club with expulsion following a series of pitch invasions and violent outbreaks. What was the club to do? Perimeter fencing? Increased stewarding? Not quite.

Chairman Alexandra Cringus came up with the innovative concept of creating a moat surrounding the pitch, packed with fully grown crocodiles. "This is not a joke," insisted Cringus. "We can get crocodiles easily enough and feed them on meat from the local abattoir. The ditch is planned to be wide enough that no one could manage to jump over it. Anyone who attempted to do so would have to deal with the crocs. I think that the problem of fans running on to the pitch will be solved once and for all."

Hmm. But what of players tumbling off the field and into the watering hole? Cringus planned to create the moat far enough from the pitch in order to prevent said calamity, yet not forgetting about the crocs; electric pipes were to be installed in the water to keep it heated during cold weather. The last we heard of the tale was that local authorities were considering the club's proposal.

"After reading about the amusing tale of Mario Zagallo and Zico taking Romario to court for painting their faces on his bar's toilet doors, I got to wondering if there have ever been any stranger lawsuits in football."

Before we press on, it would be remiss of us not to revisit the Romario story. Back in 1998, after he was axed from Zagallo's World Cup squad, Romario decided to have the toilet doors at his Cafe do Gol sports bar painted with a cartoon depiction of the national manager sitting on a toilet. Zagallo's, er, number two Zico didn't escape mockery either: he was depicted on another door with a loo roll in his hand. Zagallo launched a lawsuit, stating that "the cartoons are personal revenge for him [Romario] being dropped from the national team". Justice officials subsequently ordered the removal of the images and the doors of Romario's bar were taken away. Zagallo also received damages.

Equally lacking in humour were Michael Ballack and Oliver Kahn after German erotic retailer Beate Uhse attempted to cash in on World Cup fever in 2006 by launching a special line of 17cm vibrators. Three went by the names of 'Michael B', 'Ollie K' and 'David B'. "This is a clear violation of image rights," raged Kahn's lawyer. "We will take action." Despite the company's protestation that "we never had any intention to make a connection between the vibrators on sale in our shops with them [the players]", a judge forced Beate Uhse to pay Kahn and Ballack €50,000 and remove the items from sale.

"A friend regaled me with a tale that included the rather random fact that John Hartson once stole a sheep, but I have no means to check the veracity of the story. Say it ain't so."

Sadly, it isn't just defenders, scales and Eyal Berkovic who have been given a fright during Hartson's career, but also our woolly four-legged friends. "I was at Luton and two of my Swansea mates, Jason Wright and Kevin

Davis, came up for some fun," Hartson told FourFourTwo. "We got absolutely lashed and, at about three in the morning, we found the minibus that was to take us back to my place. On the way, we stopped beside a field and stole a sheep that was minding her own business, threw her in the back of the van and then drove on home for a sleep. There was understandable pandemonium in the morning. I had a hangover and I'd completely forgotten about the sheep, which was roaming around the back garden in a state of some distress. We bundled her back in the van and dropped her off in the first field we found with sheep in it. Somehow we got away with it."

"I read an answer in an old Knowledge column stating that one-time Southampton player CB Fry was once 'famously offered the throne of Albania'. Could you please detail how this unlikely incident happened?"

One-time Southampton player? It doesn't quite do Charles Burgess Fry justice given that he represented England at football, captained Sussex and England at cricket, and also equalled the world long jump record (7.17m in 1893), while excelling in the 100 yards sprint. But there's more. Iain Wilton, author of *CB Fry – An English Hero*, wrote: "Fry was much more than a sportsman. In fact, he was a novelist, journalist and friend to politicians on the left. He

R23338

was offered the throne of Albania but decided he hadn't quite enough money for the post."

Why did Albania offer him the role? Well, at the end of the Great War, Albania came under Italy's power. The Italians opted against garrisoning the country and instead granted it full independence under the Treaty of London in 1920. Serbia attempted to invade almost immediately, although heavy fighting drove their forces back. A suitably neutral leader was required, which is where Fry came in.

By now a speechwriter for former cricket team-mate and one of India's League of Nations representatives, Prince Ranjitsinjhi, Fry was approached in Geneva. "I accepted on the nail," Fry later wrote, somewhat portentously adding: "I was willing to be king of any willing nation." As mentioned, however, money was an issue; the Albanians required a man with an annual income of no less than £10,000 and Fry neither earned this nor could raise such an amount. Eventually, the country's president Ahmet Zogu seized power and was crowned King Zog I in 1928. Fry flirted with fascism, met Hitler, failed to crack Hollywood and died aged 84 in 1956.

"I remember reading about a match being played in an African cup competition (I think) where both teams were trying to score own goals in order to try to make/try to prevent the game from going into extra-time and being won on a golden goal. Does anyone know the exact details of this?"

It might sound like a myth, but it's (almost) 100% true. The crazy events described took place in a Shell Caribbean Cup match between Barbados and Grenada in 1994. Going into the last preliminary group game, Barbados needed to beat Grenada by two goals to qualify for the final stages. Anything less and Grenada went through. So far, so simple. Except that the organisers had decided that, in the case of extra-time, a golden goal would count as two goals.

You don't have to be Einstein to work out what happened next: Barbados raced into a 2-0 lead before Grenada made it 2-1 with seven minutes remaining. The Bajans were heading out unless they scored a goal; any goal. Fortunately for them, with three minutes left, defender Sealy did just that – only not in the right net. His deliberate own goal made it 2-2 and propelled the game into extra-time. Now, farcically, Grenada needed to score a goal (at either end) to go through. Cue frantic defending of both penalty areas by Barbados until the final whistle. Such dubious shenanigans were rewarded, however, when Barbados scored the golden goal – this time in Grenada's net – four minutes into extra-time to win the match 3-2 (or 4-2 according to the rules of the tournament) and qualify for the next stage, where they were subsequently knocked out.

However this isn't the only example of a blatant own goal being scored to further a team's ambitions: it also happened in the infamous 1998 Tiger Cup game between Thailand and Indonesia. Both teams had already secured their progression to the semis, but the winner of the game would face fancied hosts Vietnam, while the losers would meet Singapore. Having grudgingly contrived to be drawing 2-2 in the dying minutes, Indonesia's captain Mursyid Effendi had enough, collecting the ball inside his own penalty box, swivelling and driving the ball into his own net. Justice was served, mind, when both teams lost in the last four, before being fined $40,000 and given three-month suspensions for "violating the spirit of the game". Effendi's reward was a lifetime ban.

Even better, however, is the tale of the former Madagascan champions Stade Olympique L'Emyrne, narrowly beaten 149-0 in a league game after an incredible fit of pique against AS Adema in October 2002. Angry at what he perceived to be biased refereeing in a previous game, the Stade coach Zaka Be orchestrated a protest from the stands, telling his players to keep scoring own goal after own goal after, etc and so on. Bemused Adema players simply stood aghast as Stade repeatedly knocked the ball into their own net. The Malagasy Football Federation (FMF) was understandably miffed, suspending Be for three years and handing down season-long bans to the Stade goalkeeper and Madagascar captain Mamisoa Razafindrakoto, and players Manitranirina Andrianiaina, Nicolas Rakotoarimanana and Dominique Rakotonandrasana. "I certainly think it's a world record," said the FA's historian David Barber. "I've heard of a local league game in Nottingham that finished 50-2 and there was a 43-0 in an Austrian regional game before the second world war – but nothing this big."

"I'm sick of people taking the mickey out of Sepp Blatter for saying female footballers should wear tighter shorts. Weren't there also some German politicians who reckoned the men should spend more time with their tops off?"

There certainly were. Green party MPs Evelin Schönhut-Keil and Margareta Wolf got rather carried away after seeing Cristiano Ronaldo booked for baring his torso after scoring at Euro 2004, and ended up launching a national campaign to make it legal for players to take off their shirts. "Get rid of the yellow card and instead let players show their athletic torsos," wrote the pair in an open letter to the German Football Association. "We can't understand how the voluntary showing of a gorgeous male chest can be objectionable." They subsequently also threw their weight behind a petition to Fifa demanding much the same thing but, unsurprisingly, were completely ignored by both bodies.

"Did I dream it, or did I really read about Diego Maradona enhancing his reputation by once sticking it to George W Bush? I'm sure he called him 'garbage' or something like that. Why?"

It actually happened during Dubya's trip to Buenos Aires for the Summit of the Americas in 2005. Maradona had learned of Bush's impending arrival and made a pledge to lead the protests during an interview with Fidel Castro on his La Noche del Diez (The Night of the Number 10) television programme. "In Argentina, there are people who are against Bush being there," he said. "I am the first. He did us a lot of harm. As far as I'm concerned, he is a murderer; he looks down on us and tramples over us. I am going to lead that march along with my daughter."

The Guardian's account from November 5 described the protest. "The tone was struck by Maradona, who wore a 'Stop Bush' T-shirt to an anti-Bush 'counter-summit' that drew some 4,000 protesters from around the world and easily eclipsed the official summit in the public's attention. 'I'm proud as an Argentine to repudiate the presence of this human trash, George Bush,' said Maradona."

A self-confessed fan of Venezuela's president, Hugo Chávez, and the former Cuban leader Fidel Castro, Maradona maintained his US-antagoniser role last year by stating his desire to meet the Iranian president, Mahmoud Ahmadinejad. "I've already met Fidel and Chavez . . . now I need to meet your president," he told an Iranian diplomat, before giving him a signed football shirt. "I'm there with the people of Iran, really with all my heart."

"I was wondering if a child mascot or ballboy has ever been sent off during a professional game?"

Look no further than Real Betis' 2006 La Liga game at home to Atlético Madrid. With Betis clinging to a 1-0 advantage as the game entered six minutes of added-time, referee Miguel Ángel Ayza Gámez became incensed by the ballboys' refusal to return the ball (allegedly following orders from club officials). After the Atlético players complained, Ayza Gámez's patience eventually wilted, brandishing red cards to all 14 of them. Betis did have previous, though: following Chelsea's 1-0 Champions League defeat at the Manuel Ruiz de Lopera earlier that season, Jose Mourinho claimed that strange things began happening once his side fell behind. "The ballboys disappeared, making it very difficult for us," he harrumphed.

But these are not the only cases of pint-sized pests. Early in 2008, Enyimba were playing host to Nigerian rivals Wikki Tourists of Bauchi when the away side grabbed what appeared to be a last-gasp winner. Just then, a ballboy – stood adjacent to the Enyimba goalpost – threw a spare ball on to the field, prompting the referee to disallow the goal. In 2001, a Ghanaian ballboy ran on during a game to attack the referee, while another provoked the Malaga defender Vicente Valcarce into hitting him in the same year. And the Peru international goalkeeper Juan Flores was hauled off to the local nick after hospitalising ballboy Freddy Caoquira Ccalla, who repeatedly called him a "*maricón*" (faggot), during Cienciano's 2007 defeat at Total Clean. The boy was referring to a video that purported to show Flores getting up close and personal with two male friends in a bar. "If I am seen with a woman, I'm a womaniser; if I'm seen with a man, I'm a *maricón*," complained Flores.

Even cheekier, however, was one touchline troublemaker behind the goal during a 2006 Paulista Football Federation (FPF) Cup clash in Brazil between Santacruzense and Atlético Sorocaba. With the match finely poised at 1-1 in the final minute, a Santacruzense player shot into the side-netting; the aforementioned ballboy picked up the ball, placed it back on to the pitch and calmly sidefooted into the net. Before the goalkeeper could restart play, hapless referee Silvia Regina de Oliveira awarded the goal, much to the astonishment of both teams. "I should have trusted my own vision, but the linesman kept insisting it was a goal," Oliveira later apologised, but the damage had been done. The FPF suspended her, but the goal stood.

"Following the 2006 scandal in Italy, I got to wondering what the earliest ever example of match-fixing is?"

It took place a whopping 106 years earlier and involved the Burnley goalkeeper 'Happy' Jack Hillman. On the final day of the First Division season, and with his team needing to beat Nottingham Forest to avoid relegation, Hillman was alleged to have offered the opposition £2 a head to "take it easy". He upped his offer to £5 at half-time, by which point Burnley were trailing 2-0. The Clarets eventually lost 4-0 and went down to the Second Division before being hauled before the Football League. Hillman admitted speaking to Forest players, but denied trying to bribe them, instead claiming he'd only been joking. It didn't wash with the FA, which chose to set an example by banning him from the game for one year. As a result, Hillman lost a year's wages and a benefit to boot.

"My flatmate and I were in the pub last week discussing the more unusual fans of our teams. In this discussion he claimed that the late Pope John Paul II supported his team, Fulham, and that in his younger days as a priest he had actually attended a Fulham game. Is there any truth in this?"

Throughout his long and pious life, Pope John Paul II worshipped only one God. But when it came to football teams, he was much freer with his affections. For the pontiff, a handy goalkeeper in his youth, had ties to at least six sides – including Liverpool, Barcelona and

Fulham. His alleged support of the latter, in particular, has journeyed from urban myth to apparent fact – with local legend having it that John Paul II stood on the terraces at Craven Cottage in the 1930s when he was studying as a priest in Roehampton. Sadly, the story is untrue – for one thing, the Pope, born in 1920, wasn't ordained until 1946.

(An aside: when the Daily Star reported his support for the Cottagers as fact – and cunningly doctored a photo of his holiness holding a Fulham scarf to illustrate the story – the paper was reported to the Press Complaints Commission and forced to apologise.)

The story does not end there, mind. In 1999, Ken Myers of the supporters' group, the Fulham Independent Fanline, phoned the Vatican to ask about the rumours, later telling reporters: "I'd heard the Pope was a fan so, as it was Easter, I thought I'd give him a ring. I couldn't believe it when I got through to his press spokesman. This guy even knew we were playing Wigan and was happy to talk about it." Pope John Paul II's special envoy, Kieron Conroy, was a bit less forward on the subject, however. "The Pope wishes Fulham fans all the best," he said. "He has written before hoping Fulham's fortunes would be reversed and offers his support, such as he can give it."

John Paul II was also a keen Liverpool fan, at least according to the club's Polish keeper, Jerzy Dudek. "I spoke to a couple of guys who are very close to the Pope, and they told me he is always watching our games and he is always thinking of me when Liverpool play," he revealed in 2004 after the pontiff had been introduced to the Poland national team.

This list of clubs doesn't end there, however. The pontiff was also an honorary member of several European clubs, including – bizarrely – both the German side Schalke (a strongly Catholic club that signed him up in 1987) and their bitter local rivals Borussia Dortmund (which he "joined" in 2005). He also had a lifelong Barcelona membership card – No 108,000 – which he was given after performing mass at Camp Nou, in front of 120,000 people, in November 1982.

But despite all these fanciful affiliations, most Poles will tell you that John Paul II really only had eyes for one team – Cracovia Kraków. The evidence fits: he was born 30 miles from Kraków, undertook his university and seminary studies in the city, and watched the team from the terraces in his youth. That support seems to have lingered until the end: in 2005 he granted the team's players and staff a private audience at the Vatican. After giving them his blessing, he assured the team he still supported them. They weren't alone, that's all.

"Have they ever used an actual hat for the FA Cup draw? If so, when was it last used and what kind of hat was it?"

Early draws really did involve headwear; a top hat covered by a handkerchief, to be precise. It was filled with pieces of paper bearing the names of the clubs, with a member of the FA committee delicately lifting a corner of the handkerchief to draw the ties. Bryon Butler's *Official Illustrated History of the FA Cup* is the only source of information regarding this arcane ritual; until the first radio coverage of the draw in December 1935 it had been "barred and bolted against all unofficial comers" – including the press. By then, the bag-and-ball arrangement was in place. Indeed, the then FA secretary, Sir Stanley Rous, was asked by the BBC to rattle the balls in the bag for dramatic effect.

David Barber, the FA's historian, suggests that the top hat and handkerchief met their demise in the drive for modernisation, sometime around 1914. Nevertheless, phrases such as "in the hat for the next round" will always have their roots in the actual routine of the draw.

"I vaguely recall a Match of the Day FA Cup special some years ago when a female reporter abruptly broke off her summary of a match and then angrily swore. If it did indeed happen, who was the offending journalist?"

Despite a host of names being bandied around, we've finally managed to track down the culprit from the FA Cup first-round show of 1998. Step forward ... Sue Thearle. An anonymous source at MotD told us that, during highlights of Basingstoke Town's 2-1 defeat at home to Bournemouth, "[Sue] made a mistake on the voiceover and swore so they did another take. But the editor didn't put the machines into edit and did a 'preview' (basically a practice where you can hear the new version, but it doesn't commit to tape so the old version was still there) and they thought he had recorded it. They then rushed it off to air without checking it through and sent it out for all to hear." Ever the professional, host Des Lynam failed to bat an eyelid upon his subsequent piece-to-camera.

Fortunately, by the time the early-morning Sunday replay of the programme went to air, the correct version was broadcast. However, if you want to relive the memorable moment in all its glory ("The Ryman League side gave the visitors a second-half . . . shit!"), then YouTube has all the gory evidence.

"What is the longest run of league games undefeated in world football?"

Milan enjoyed an unbeaten Serie A run that lasted a massive 58 games and took place between May 19 1991 and March 21 1993, before they eventually lost 1-0 at home to Parma. That, however, is still a long way short of Tunisia's Espérance (85 games between 1997 to 2001) and Steaua Bucharest, who used their lofty position as Romania's Army team to good effect, employing the nation's finest players and remaining unbeaten in Divizia A for 104 matches between 1986 and 1989.

Pipping Steaua to the world record, though, are Asec Abidjan of the Ivory Coast. Boasting a team packed with Ivorian internationals, Asec went 108 matches without defeat between 1989 and 1994. When their winning streak eventually came to an end – via a 2-1 defeat at the hands of SO Armée – the backlash was immediate and severe: they crushed their next opponents 11-0.

"Is it true that a one-armed man has won the World Cup?"

The Uruguayan striker Héctor Castro is that man, having lost the lower part of his left limb in an unfortunate carpentry accident at the age of 13. Not that this swayed him from his dream, mind, as he went on to represent his country and even score a last-minute clinching goal in the 4-2 final win over Argentina in 1930.

"Has a player-manager ever placed himself on the transfer list or even sold himself to another club?"

Ivan Broadis, born in Poplar, east London, in 1922, is one notable example, although due to a Football League administration error (his signature was misread), he was known as Ivor. After a spell as a wartime RAF navigator, his early playing career took in amateur appearances for Finchley, Northfleet, Finchley again, Tottenham, and Millwall, before he became the youngest player-manager ever at Carlisle – in 1946 – at the tender age of 23.

"Although his time as manager of the club could be regarded as being average, Broadis laid the foundations for the future, and when he left in January 1949 [replaced by one Bill Shankly], United were in a far healthier state than when he had taken over," explains an article on the Cumbrians' official website. "Still registered as a player, he sold himself to Sunderland for £18,000 [a figure agreed by the board], claiming that it was in the best interests of the club that he leave, providing Carlisle with suitable financial reimbursement for the transfer. The fans were not convinced, but accepted his move out of respect for the money it produced."

Ivor's playing career took him on to Manchester City, Newcastle, back to Carlisle and finally Queen of the South, while he also accrued 14 caps for England and played in the 1954 World Cup finals. He hung up his boots in 1962, choosing to take up a career in journalism, reporting for the Carlisle Evening News and Star, the Northern Echo and also the Observer.

"I seem to recall reading that Luton's former Danish international, Lars Elstrup, went off the rails somewhat after he retired. He found religion, but what then?"

Ah yes, the strange case of Lars Elstrup. Well, he did indeed become a religious revolutionary, adopting the name Darando ("the river that flows into the sea") after joining up with Englishman Michael Barnett's radical Wild Goose Company on a settlement in his homeland. "Michael has helped me and is my master," confirmed Elstrup by way of explanation in 1995. "We meditate several times a day and look into ourselves. I don't need anybody outside this centre!" However, things eventually turned sour at the commune and, according to a report in the Sun, the final straw came when he was denied visiting rights to his pet dachshund. "I saw no reason to carry on," said the Dane. "I tried to hang myself and cut my wrists but I couldn't go through with it. I lay in bed for 18 hours a day for two years."

There were further sightings of Elstru ... sorry, Darando, notably by a crack team of Observer hacks. As a 2000 report in the newspaper described, "most recently he was spotted in the middle of the busiest pedestrian shopping street in Copenhagen circled by a rope, waving his penis at passers-by. 'In some respects,' he explained, 'I do this to provoke people. I like experiencing people's reactions. Some might take my message to be "sod off" and others an offer of sex. I am very aware of people's reactions and I love the fact that people recognise me as Lars Elstrup.' When he tested the theory by repeating the act for the female shoppers of Odense, he was heckled, lost his temper, slapped a laughing schoolboy, wrestled a police officer, was arrested and finally expelled by the Geese."

According to the same newspaper's Said and Done column, Elstrup's final media appearance to date was thus: "Nine months on – after legal action – he turned up in the park to play football with NME and Loaded writers. He went on to score five in his underpants – telling team-mates 'drink more water – yellow piss is for losers'. After the match, someone asked if he fancied a pint. 'No,' said Lars. 'Pussy,' and strode off towards the West End. No one's seen him since."

"Following Lille's ludicrous attempt to leave the pitch when losing to Manchester United [in the 2006-07 Champions League], are there any similar instances of a team walking off during a game?"

It's nothing new. In fact, such behaviour can be traced back as far as December 12 1891 when Burnley's game at home to Blackburn had to be abandoned because the Rovers players left the field ... complaining of the numbing cold. Andrew Ward's book, *Football's Strangest Matches*, recalls that shortly after the interval all of Blackburn's outfield players returned to the changing room, leaving only their goalkeeper Herby Arthur on the pitch. Upon the resumption of play, Arthur managed to, successfully, appeal for offside. With no one to pass to from the subsequent free-kick, he began time-wasting and it wasn't long before the referee had abandoned the game.

More famously, the 1982 World Cup match between France and Kuwait was temporarily suspended by handbags, acrimony, a walk-off and the intervention of royalty. With France leading 3-1, Alain Giresse cantered past bewildered Kuwaiti defenders to hammer home a fourth, but as the tiny midfielder wheeled away in celebration, the Kuwaitis complained that they hadn't tried to stop him, claiming they had heard a whistle and assumed the Russian referee, Miroslav Stupar, had blown to halt play. Prince Fahd Al-Ahmed Al-Jaber, the president of the Kuwaiti Football Association, threatened to withdraw his team if the goal wasn't disallowed. Stupar eventually agreed to chalk it off, but he never officiated another World Cup game. Justice was done when Maxime Bossis scored in the final minute, while further punishment was meted out in the shape of a £6,500 fine.

Whereas the prince's plan lacked cunning, Chilean goalkeeper Roberto Rojas's was masterful in its sheer deviousness. With his team trailing 2-0 against Brazil in a 1989 World Cup qualifier, a firecracker landed in the penalty area, prompting Rojas to fling himself dramatically to the floor. Holding his forehead, he covertly removed a razor blade from his glove and slashed at his scalp. As Rojas left the field on a stretcher, his team-mates sparked a riot, before leaving the field and forcing the referee to abandon the game. He hadn't counted on television cameras catching him red-handed, though, and Fifa kicked Chile out of the tournament (and banned them from the next one), excluding Rojas from football for life. The woman who threw the flare was signed up by Playboy Brazil and Rojas eventually had his ban lifted in 2001. "At 43, I'm unlikely to play again," he admitted after the decision. "But at least this pardon will cleanse my soul."

The fastest walk-off, however, must surely have come in the 1999 Cairo derby, where Al-Ahly's game with Zamalek (played at the neutral 120,000-seater

International Stadium due to security concerns) was done and dusted within two minutes. French referee Marc Batta had been drafted in to handle the game, but his decision to dismiss Zamalek's Ayman Abdel Aziz for an early tackle from behind resulted in the rest of his team-mates storming off the field in protest and refusing to continue. Al-Ahly eventually won the game and the Egyptian FA fined Zamalek, who were also taken to court by four angry fans who accused them of throwing the game.

"Has any club ever been cruel enough to give their manager the boot on Christmas Day?"

Heartless as it sounds, a club *has* been known to sack its manager on Jesus's birthday, and they were even brave enough to ruin the festivities for one José Mário dos Santos Mourinho Félix. "I was nine or 10 years old and my father [Félix] was sacked on Christmas Day," recalled the former Chelsea manager during an interview in 2004. "He was a manager, the results had not been good, he lost a game on December 22 or 23. On Christmas Day, the telephone rang and he was sacked in the middle of our lunch. So I know all about the ups and downs of football. I know that one day I will be sacked."

"Are there any players that have actually come out and just admitted: 'I moved for the money'?"

When Hibernian's Scotland striker Garry O'Connor moved to Lokomotiv Moscow in 2006, the striker was honest enough to admit it was all part of a greater plan to retire early with some serious savings in the bank. "I can set my family up for life," said O'Connor about the move. "If I was single and never had [fiancee] Lisa and [son] Josh I maybe wouldn't have made the move to Russia. But I signed a five-year contract and I have other ambitions to play in England, Italy, Spain or France." Within 15 months, O'Connor had secured a transfer to Birmingham.

Pint-sized Canadian forward Tomasz Radzinski was similarly straightforward in his attitude to leaving Anderlecht in 2001. "I'd love to sign for Everton," he claimed, shortly before joining the Toffees. "They are offering me a wonderful four-year deal, I could earn three times as much as I do now at Anderlecht. I know Everton are not a top club." Chris Waddle too displayed admirable candour when explaining his switch from Tottenham to Marseille in 1989. "I just had to accept," said Waddle, "because of what it offered my family for the future." And when Lars Bohinen ditched Nottingham Forest for the brighter lights of Jack Walker's Blackburn in 1995, at least he had the good grace to acknowledge he was moving purely for the cash. "It was like winning the lottery," he beamed. "I was able to negotiate the kind of contract that would otherwise have been way beyond my reach."

However, no one was in it for the money as much as a certain Winston Bogarde, whose four starts in almost four years with Chelsea earned him roughly £8.2m. No wonder he shamelessly refused to leave Stamford Bridge when they were so eager to shed him from their swollen wage bill. "Why should I throw £15m away when it is already mine?" charmed Bogarde in his autobiography, the catchily titled *Winston Bogarde: This Black Man Bows For No One.* "At the moment I signed it was in fact my money, my contract – both sides agreed whole-heartedly. This world is about money, so when you are offered those millions you take them. Few people will ever earn so much. I may be one of the worst buys in the history of the Premiership, but I don't care."

"Did the Belgian striker Gilles de Bilde really miss a game for his club because his dog had died?"

Well, it was reported that Willebroek Meerhof, De Bilde's employers, were planning disciplinary action against him for taking the match off in bereavement, although this wasn't the first time the animal enthusiast's relationship with his pets had got him into trouble. Shortly after arriving at Sheffield Wednesday in 1999, De Bilde was the subject of an attempted News of the

World exposé; the newspaper claimed to have proof that he had smuggled his two pet dobermans – Zico and Diego – past customs illegally without having them go through quarantine. De Bilde, who had publicly campaigned for a European ban on dog and cat fur in the past, denied the allegations, insisting the dogs he kept in his English home belonged to a friend. "Quarantine laws are shit laws because they affect dogs' health," fumed De Bilde. "That's not a good thing."

However, it wasn't long before canines got him into more trouble with Paul Jewell [Wednesday's manager at the time] just over a year later, after he had demanded a move back up to the Premiership. "I fixed him up with three months on loan at Aston Villa," said Jewell. "But when I called him in to tell him, he said: 'I've got a problem. I've got nobody to look after my dogs if I go there.' I said, 'Give us your house keys, I'll feed the bloody dogs.' That was the sort of thing I was up against."

"I seem to remember a fox invading an Old Firm game when Gazza was at Rangers. Have there been any similar animal-related incidents?"

Plenty is the answer to that one, as many a hapless steward will tell you. The incident in question occurred back in November 1996, when the Parkhead pitch was encroached upon by a bushy tailed invader. Referee

Hugh Dallas was forced to delay a Celtic corner as the intruder gave several players the slip before dashing back into the crowd. "We were very impressed with the pace of the fox," admitted Celtic's public relations manager, Peter McLean. "It still hasn't been caught. We don't know how it got in and how it escaped. We have even been given the brush-off by its agent." The 'Old Furm' game ended 1-0 in Rangers' favour, by the way.

Other instances of animal gatecrashers include: the duck that gave legendary German goalkeeper Sepp Maier the slip during Bayern Munich's Bundesliga match with VfL Bochum in 1976; 'Squirrel Regis', who wandered on to the Highbury field during Arsenal's final European game there against Villarreal in 2006; and the pheasant released in Camp Nou during Barcelona's 2002 Champions League game with Panathinaikos. Sadly, an embarrassed steward took his frustration out on the bird when he finally caught up, ruthlessly booting it into the next life, before dragging the limp bird away.

A dog named Bryn was given a more salubrious send-off after he helped save Torquay from relegation to the Conference in 1987. Trailing 2-1 at home to Crewe on the final day of the season, the Gulls were staring down the barrel ... until their canine saviour arrived. Patrolling the touchline with his handler, police dog Bryn took a chunk out of Torquay's Jim McNichol when he came too near. It took four minutes for McNichol to be patched up and it was in the fourth minute of injury-time that Torquay's Paul Dobson grabbed an equaliser. Rivals Lincoln were beaten at Swansea, meaning Torquay, incredibly, stayed up on goal difference. After his death, Bryn was stuffed and put on display inside the Plainmoor boardroom.

Not that animal interlopers are always so helpful. A far more unfortunate incident befell goalkeeper Chic Brodie, whose professional career came to an end in November 1970 when playing for Brentford at Colchester. A dog (believed to be a terrier) ran on to the pitch in chase of a long ball, causing inevitable mayhem. As Brodie waited to collect a backpass, the mutt flew at him, knocking the Scotsman to the ground; he was stretchered off, having shattered his kneecap, and never played football again. A philosophical Brodie later reflected: "The dog might have been a small one, but it just happened to be a solid one."

Most incredibly, though, was an insect invasion in 2008. Santacruzense player Marcos Paulo was forced to leave the pitch when he, quite literally, was caught with ants in his pants during a São Paulo state championship match. "I only rolled on the grass for three seconds to win the foul," moaned Paulo. "I got up, then started to feel shit. I looked down and my chest, sides and legs were black. I was screaming but the ref didn't understand and tried to book me. They were in my pants and right up me so I jumped in a puddle then ran to the showers screaming. The players now call me the Ant. It hurt like hell."

"Was Taffarel, the Brazil keeper at the 1998 World Cup, playing as a striker for some remote European team prior to the tournament?"

The church of Preziosissimo Sangue ("the most precious blood") in Reggiana was the "remote" team in question. Taffarel had been loaned out to Reggiana by Parma, who had no room in their line-up for the Brazilian owing to foreign player quotas. Time passed and again Taffarel found himself on the sidelines. "I was unemployed for seven months," he explained. "Imagine, a world champion without a club! It's unbelievable. I ended up playing for my church team, just for fun. I even played centre-forward for a while and scored 15 goals in seven games. It wouldn't be fair to the other teams for me to play as a goalkeeper." Atlético Mineiro soon brought him back to Brazil and he regained his spot in the national team in time to help them reach the World Cup final in Paris.

"I vaguely recall hearing that Shay Given has a special bottle of water he puts in his goal before every match. Is this true?"

According to the man himself, it is. Prior to every game he plays, the Republic of Ireland keeper places a vial of Lourdes holy water at the back of his goal as a lucky charm. "I carry it in my kit bag and it goes everywhere with me," he told the Irish News of the World in 2002. Apparently, the water carries with it powers that many Roman Catholics ascribe to the Lourdes spring, where apparitions of the Virgin Mary first appeared in 1858. Given also takes a picture of his late mother wherever he goes. "He's been doing it since he was small," revealed his father Seamus. "I don't know how much he remembers her because he was so young when she died, but he doesn't want to forget about her."

It won't come as any real surprise that goalkeepers are as superstitious as they come, and myths abound that Arsenal's will never wear a brand new shirt unless it has already been washed. Apparently, this dates back to the Gunners' 1927 FA Cup final defeat to Cardiff, when Dan Lewis blamed a greasy new woollen top for the mistake that led to the only goal of the game. Prior to this, the Woolwich Arsenal keeper Leigh Richmond Roose (cited by the Daily Mail in 1905 as one of the capital's most eligible bachelors, no less) had a similar clothing ritual. Legend has it that Roose played every match with an unwashed "lucky" black-and-green Aberystwyth top underneath his jersey. "Roose is one of the cleanest custodians we have, but he apparently is a trifle superstitious about his football garments, for he seldom seems to trouble the charwoman with them," read one March 1904 account in Bolton's Cricket and Football Field. "Considerable amusement was created at Stoke on Saturday and again at Liverpool on Monday, when it was noticed that Roose alone failed to turn out in spick and span garments. His pants, we should say, carried about them the marks of many a thrilling contest."

But surely nobody can outdo John Terry in the superstition stakes. He admitted having "about 50", including using the same spot in the Chelsea car park, listening to the same Usher CD before games, sitting in the same seat on the team bus, and wearing a pair of Frank Lampard's old shinpads he's had for 10 years.

"Have any players ever used a corner flag, a goalpost or an advertising hoarding to attack an opponent?"

Step forward Canada's Paul Peschisolido, who flipped a corner flag into an El Salvador player's face during a World Cup qualifier in 1997, and duly picked up a red card for his troubles. "I was kicked a few times and the referee wasn't giving anything, while every challenge we made seemed to result in a foul," explained Peschisolido afterwards. "I was getting very annoyed and frustrated so I decided to elbow one of their players. It was right in the corner and in fact I elbowed the corner flag into his face."

Martin Keown managed the next best thing in January 2002, chucking a corner flag into the stands during Arsenal's 1-1 league draw at Elland Road. Early in the game Keown conceded a corner; as he got up he grabbed the flag and casually lobbed it behind him into the front rows of fans. Despite uproar from the supporters, the FA eventually decided he had not intended to hit them, and did not enforce any punishment.

Sadly there were no such exciting tales regarding advertising hoardings, though the 2007 match between Orlando Pirates and Black Leopards in South Africa's Premier Soccer League surely warrants a mention. With the game in mid-flow, heavy winds suddenly sent a number of hoardings flying across the pitch, taking out a linesman and several players in a matter of seconds. Thankfully no one was seriously injured.

"I read that Philippe Troussier has managed six different national sides (South Africa, Nigeria, Ivory Coast, Burkina Faso, Japan and Qatar). Can anyone match that?"

They can and they have. In a career spanning almost 24 years in charge of national teams, Velibor "Bora" Milutinović has managed six different sides: Mexico, Costa Rica, United States, Nigeria, China, Honduras and Jamaica. But leaving Milutinović well and truly in the shade is Rudi Gutendorf. Incredibly, his management career lasted 53 years and took in 17 national managers' jobs (and an amazing 54 in all) with ... Chile, Bolivia, Venezuela, Trinidad & Tobago, Grenada, Antigua, Botswana, Australia, New Caledonia, Nepal, Tonga, Tanzania, Ghana, Nepal again (but we won't count that), Fiji, Zimbabwe, Mauritius and Rwanda. Oh, and he also took charge of the Iranian and Chinese Olympic teams in 1988 and 1992, respectively. When asked once why he had managed in so many different countries, the German replied: "One cannot conserve excitement."

"A couple of years ago I stumbled across what looked like Garth Crooks presenting Newsnight. I'm still, to this day, unsure of whether it was a bad dream or it actually happened. What's the deal?"

Close, but no cigar: what you were watching was indeed on BBC2, but it was everyone's (OK, the odd person's) favourite questioner hosting Despatch Box, a late-night politics show. It transpires that Garth used his spare time as a player at Tottenham to study politics at college. Along with this and his BBC Sport work, another string to his broadcasting bow has been the "discussion-cum-record" radio show he hosted on Greater London Radio, Garth Crooks in Conversation.

"After watching Thierry Henry and Robert Pires shambolically screw up a two-man penalty, I was wondering if the Johan Cruyff/Jesper Olsen incident was the only previous example of it?"

Well, despite Henry admitting to having taken his inspiration from the Ajax duo's famous spot-kick in 1982, there are three far earlier examples of the cheeky 'tap penalty'. On November 21 1964, Plymouth Argyle beat Manchester City 3-2 in a Division Two game at Home Park. The winning goal came from Mike Trebilcock: after the referee gave the Pilgrims a penalty, Johnny Newman tapped the ball sideways, enabling Trebilcock to race in and fire home. However, Argyle had already employed the trick once before. Some further digging reveals that Newman was involved again – on February 6 1961, in the 5-3 League Cup fourth-round, second replay defeat to Aston Villa. This time Wilf Carter nudged the ball for Newman to run in and crash home.

Yet the nearest variation to the "two-touch" penalty can be tracked back even further; all the way to June 5 1957, in fact, when Belgium entertained Iceland in a World Cup qualifying tie. Already leading 6-1, Belgium were awarded a 44th-minute penalty. Up stepped Rik Coppens, but instead of firing towards Björgvin Hermannsson in the Iceland goal, Coppens nonchalantly passed to team-mate André Piters, who returned the favour, enabling the former to score past a stunned

Hermannsson. The match ended 8-3 and Coppens went on to be voted 73rd on a list of all-time great Belgians.

"Did the father of Gil Scott-Heron, jazz radical, play for Celtic in the fifties (maybe sixties) and, if so, for how long and to what effect?"

Giles Heron began his football career in the Canadian Air Force and went on to play for the Detroit Wolverines, Chicago Sting and Detroit Corinthians. He signed for Celtic in 1951 after scoring twice in an open trial. Heron would only play one league game for the Hoops, however, although he made four appearances in the Scottish League Cup, scoring two goals. He was released by the club in 1952 and went on to enjoy short spells with Third Lanark and Kidderminster Harriers.

His son – who made his name in 1970 with the superb jazz-funk polemic The Revolution Will Not Be Televised – was asked about his father's exploits by Scottish magazine One. "It's a blessing from the spirits," he explained. "Like, that's the two things that Scottish folks love the most; music and football, and they got one representative from each of those from my family. Personally I support Rangers and I'm going to wear my Celtic scarf and Rangers hat when I come over."

"Looking over past European statistics I noticed a combined team of 'London' lost in the final of the first Inter-City Fairs Cup. I would be interested to know what players took part and which club they came from."

A London XI did lose the 1958 Inter-City Fairs Cup final, during a rare period of enforced harmony in the English capital. Rules stated that only one team per city could enter the competition [a forerunner to the Uefa Cup], hence the need for a London XI. Anyway, having seen off Basle and Frankfurt in the group stage and then Lausanne-Sports in the semis, London faced Barcelona in the final. Jim Langley's 88th-minute penalty salvaged a 2-2 draw in the first leg at Stamford Bridge, but in the return game, almost two months later, the Catalans stormed to a 6-0 win.

The line-ups for the games with Barça were as follows – first leg: Jack Kelsey (Arsenal), Peter Sillett (Chelsea), Jim Langley (Fulham), Danny Blanchflower, Maurice Norman (both Tottenham Hotspur), Ken Coote (Brentford), Vic Groves (Arsenal), Jimmy Greaves (Chelsea), Bobby Smith (Tottenham Hotspur), Johnny Haynes (Fulham), George Robb (Tottenham Hotspur).

Second leg: Jack Kelsey (Arsenal), George Wright (Leyton Orient), Noel Cantwell (West Ham United), Danny Blanchflower (Tottenham Hotspur), Ken Brown (West Ham United), Dave Bowen (Arsenal), Terry Medwin

(Tottenham Hotspur), Vic Groves (Arsenal), Bobby Smith (Tottenham Hotspur), Jimmy Bloomfield (Arsenal), Jim Lewis (Chelsea).

"Is Osmo Tapio Everton Räihälä the only composer in classical music who has dedicated his work to a football team and their players?"

Remarkably, the answer is no. But before we get on to other composers, we'll let the questioner, Aki Niemi, divulge a little more information on the aforementioned Mr Räihälä: "He is a composer who gets inspiration from – among other things – football, in particular his beloved Everton. He has made a special Everton series of compositions, with pieces of art including [Nick] Chadwick Drive and Barlinnie Nine. The latter is the concluding part of the Everton series and, as its name suggests, it's dedicated to Duncan Ferguson [Barlinnie being the prison of the same name]. The premiere of Barlinnie Nine was on April 20 2005 in Helsinki, performed by the Finnish Radio Symphony Orchestra and, fittingly, later that night Duncan Ferguson scored the only goal of the game in Everton's win over Manchester United."

Spooky. But it isn't just the Toffeemen who have had beautiful music written about them. QPR fan and composer extraordinaire Michael Nyman has used the

Super Hoops as his muse. "The Final Score was composed in 1991 for a Channel 4 film directed by Matthew Whiteman, which, delightfully, allowed me to drift from the Queens Park Rangers of the present back to the golden days of the Stan Bowles-inspired team of the mid-70s," he explained. "The score is a straightforward set of variations of a four-note bass line and is anthemic enough to lift QPR immediately back into the Premier League."

Then there's the Scottish composer James McMillan, himself an avid Celtic fan, who wrote a piano concerto about the Bhoys' 1989 Cup Winners' Cup first-round defeat to Partizan Belgrade. "I was so fascinated by the misplaced energy being shown – great drives forward countered by suicidal defending," said McMillan. "I can safely say that, in the history of music, I am the only composer to write a piece inspired by the away goals rule!"

David Golightly's Symphony No1 is an opus dedicated to Middlesbrough, or, more specifically, "[chairman] Steve Gibson, the players and staff". And, as the Guardian's Ed Vulliamy wrote back in 2000, "Dmitri Shostakovich, the greatest composer of the 20th century, was a football fanatic. He was, said Maxim Gorky, 'a rabid fan. He comported himself like a little boy, leapt up, screamed and gesticulated' at matches. Shostakovich supported Leningrad Zenith; he would cut short his composing retreats in some rural idyll and return to the city for home games."

"Has a streaker ever scored? And would it count if they did?"

The self-proclaimed "world's No1 streaker", Mark Roberts from Liverpool, has "scored" at least two goals while baring all. Roberts, who has also streaked at the Super Bowl and Royal Ascot, scored in the Liverpool v Chelsea Carling Cup game at Anfield in 2000 and the 2002 Champions League final between Real Madrid and Bayer Leverkusen. At Anfield, Roberts hurdled the

perimeter fence, took a pass from Gianfranco Zola before beating the entire Chelsea defence and firing past a half-hearted Ed de Goey. His goal bonus: a magistrates court appearance and £100 fine. At Hampden Park, wearing nothing but a Tam O'Shanter and a smile, he stole the ball, ran past two defenders and found the aptly named Leverkusen keeper Hans-Jorg Butt no match for his finishing prowess.

Roberts isn't the only streaker to find the back of the net, mind. In December 1998, during an interruption in Reading's 1-0 win over Notts County, a fan ran on to the field, kissed the ground and scored past the County keeper before evading a steward and disappearing back into the crowd.

These goals didn't count because they occurred during breaks in play (both of Roberts' came during the half-time interval), but even if a streaker was to find the net during a game, it wouldn't count. In Fifa's rules of the game, Law 10, The Method of Scoring, says that a goal can only be given if no infringement has been made by the team scoring the goal. Obviously, a streaker would be an ineligible player, a team cannot field more than 11, so there would be no goal. And that's even before considering improper kit. The referee also has the power to stop the game if "an unauthorised person enters the field of play".

"What would happen if every game in the Premier League finished 0-0? Would league positions be decided alphabetically?"

It's disappointing news for Arsenal and Villa fans. If every club decided to park the bus throughout the season's fixtures in the top-flight and somehow keep them all goalless, Rule B31 would come in to play. According to the Premier League, it goes a little like this: "If at the end of the season either the league champions or the clubs to be relegated or the question of qualification for other competitions cannot be determined because two or more clubs are equal on points, goal difference and goals scored, the clubs concerned shall play off one or more decided league matches on neutral grounds, the format, timing and venue of which shall be determined by the board."

"Is it true that Australian football was once cursed by a witch doctor?"

Back in 1969, the Australian national side travelled to face Rhodesia (now Zimbabwe) as they attempted to qualify for the following year's World Cup finals in Mexico. When they heard about a witch doctor in nearby Mozambique who said he could help their cause by placing a curse on the Rhodesians, the Aussies were more than happy for him to plant some bones near one of the goalposts and do his stuff. Australia duly won 3-1, only to ignore the witch doctor's demand for £1,000. Big mistake.

The curse was duly reversed and, with the exception of qualification for the 1974 finals, Australian football plunged headlong into decades of misery. It was not until John Safran, an Australian comic, heard the story that fortunes changed. With the help of a different witchdoctor – the original one had died, presumably a grand poorer than he had hoped, in 1969 – Safran helped lift the curse in time for Australia to qualify for Germany 2006. "[It] involved us sitting in the middle of the pitch and he [the witch doctor] killed a chicken and splattered the blood all over me," explained Safran. "I then had to go to Telstra Stadium and we had to wash ourselves in some clay the witch doctor had given us." According to an article in the Sydney Morning Herald, Safran "said he had forgotten about the story until he began receiving emails from people thanking him for having lifted the curse".

"Has witchcraft ever been used at the African Cup of Nations?"

Juju played a part in the 2008 tournament: in the opening match between hosts Ghana and Guinea, several Ghana fans carried juju pots containing leaves and liquid in order – according to one, Kojo Saaka – to "scare away all devils". It seemed to work, if you believe in this sort of thing or are a journalist in need of copy to file, as Ghana's Sulley Muntari scored a last-minute screamer to win the game.

This is nothing on what happened in the 2002 semi-final between Mali and Cameroon, though, when the Cameroon coach Winfried Schafer and his goalkeeping coach, Thomas Nkono, were arrested by riot police for placing a magic charm on the pitch before the match. Or two years previously, when a Nigerian FA official skittered on to the pitch before kick-off to steal a charm which had been placed in the back of the opposition net during his country's quarter-final with Senegal. His intervention earned him a red card, but Nigeria did go on to win the game. Make of that what you will. "I believe that it [juju] does exist," Laloko later told the BBC World Service. "As an African, we have our customs and traditions." A spokesperson for the Confederation of African Football, meanwhile, told the Observer in 2002 of fears that such incidents propagate the image of Africa as a third-world continent. "We are no more willing to see witch doctors on the pitch than cannibals at the concession stands."

"Is it true that Albania once barred Celtic's defender Danny McGrain from entering the country because he had a beard?"

Very nearly, is the answer, because communist Albania frowned at all facial hair under its leader Enver Hoxha, who had made beards illegal before Celtic were due to travel for their 1979 European Cup first-round first leg tie against Partizan Tirana. The owner of a fine-follicled face-hugger himself, McGrain was understandably anxious before the trip, recalling that "there was a lot in the press about beards being banned there".

As it transpired, no one told McGrain to shave it off and he went on to play in a 1-0 defeat. "I would have done it if they had asked, but I had actually seen a few people with them," added the Celtic legend, whose side subsequently ran out 4-1 winners in the return game. "It was a little intimidating too because when we went outside there were only men in the streets and no women to be seen, but there was no bother at all."

Right-back McGrain went on to win 62 caps for Scotland, before moving into management at Arbroath, where his fancy chin-warmer came to prominence again. "I'll never forget how the fans took to Danny McGrain and his beard," recalled then chairman John Christison of the so-called 'Danny McGrain's Bearded Army'. "It was crazy – but brilliant. They would all wear their own beards and we had 700 T-shirts printed up. They sold out in three days."

"Thumbing through the history of Scottish Cup winners the other day, I noticed that no one seemed to have won the trophy in 1909. Did they have a year off? What really happened?"

You appear to have stumbled upon the story of the Hampden Riot, which resulted in the Scottish Football Association holding back the trophy. Back in 1909, Rangers and Celtic had set up another Old Firm final showdown, which went to a replay after the sides drew 2-2 in a thrilling first game. But rumours began sweeping the city that the SFA had been fixing Cup ties in a bid to ensure maximum income from replays, sparking understandable suspicion and mistrust among both sets of supporters.

That sense of paranoia peaked after the replay on April 17, which finished in a 1-1 draw; as the players left the field an announcement revealed there would be no extra-time and the thinning patience of 60,000 supporters finally ran out. Fans from both sides united to invade the pitch for more than 2½ hours, tearing up the goalposts and setting fire to the wooden barricades. Mounted police were fended off with stones and even the goalposts, while the fire brigade was also repelled by missiles and had its hoses cut. Around 50 policemen were injured as the riot eventually left the stadium and moved towards the city centre. Both clubs petitioned the SFA to have the tie abandoned and their demands were duly met when officials decided the match would not be replayed. The cup and all medals were withheld, although both clubs were compensated to the amount of £150, while Queen's Park received £500 for the damage. "I would suggest the withdrawal of all policemen from football matches," wrote one correspondent in the Glasgow Evening Times, "and substitute a regiment of soldiers with fixed bayonets."

"There's a story doing the rounds at my local that Blackpool once resorted to using a flamethrower to thaw out their frozen pitch. Would I be right to think it's total guff?"

Well, it's not quite true, but it is closer to reality than you might imagine. The winter of 1962-63 was extremely harsh, and Blackpool suffered more than most as their pitch completely froze over to the point where they couldn't play a single home game between December 15 and March 2. Some players even took to ice skating on the pitch, as revealed by the following gem, dug out of the West Lancashire Evening Gazette's archives by Seasiders historian Gerry Wolstenholme: "At Bloomfield Road Jimmy Armfield and Tony Waiters ice skated on the pitch on January 8 1963 and two days later they were joined by Barrie Martin, 'Mandy' Hill and two other players. On January 29 1963 Blackpool used a disc harrow to try to get the game against West Ham United played on February 2 1963, but that too proved ineffective and on January 30 1963 the players swept a heavy fall of snow from the pitch in a vain hope that it would be clear underneath, but the ice – one to four inches thick – was 'as formidable as ever'."

It was actually Norwich who attempted, unsuccessfully, to defrost their playing surface with the aid of fire. Their scheduled FA Cup third-round tie at home to Blackpool had been postponed 11 times, and, as the same piece of archive reveals, they were willing to try just about anything by the end. "In an attempt to get the game played, the Carrow Road pitch was treated with flamethrowers on January 22 1963 as, according to a Norwich spokesman, 'a last desperate effort'. However, they 'served no purpose whatsoever' for 'as fast as the ice melted it froze again'. An icebreaker was also used but it too proved ineffective."

Moving north of the border, there is one other notable example of unorthodox pitch preparation, as the Dundee United website explains. "The winter of 1962-63 was particularly harsh and [Dundee] United had already been denied two matches due to Tannadice being icebound," it begins. "Desperate to play a Scottish Cup tie against Albion Rovers in January 1963, United hired a tar burner of the kind used by road-layers to melt the ice. However, the predictable after-effect left the playing surface all but devoid of grass. Undaunted, the directors

FWOOSH!

ordered several lorry-loads of sand, spread it around, painted some lines on it and, astonishingly, the referee pronounced the 'pitch' playable.

"United won the tie handsomely, prompting some observers to comment that they had taken to the new surface 'like Arabs'. The supporters, however, quickly hijacked the name for themselves, the next few matches witnessing some fans wearing crude approximations of Arab headgear. The practice never became widespread until the late 70s and early 80s when it was seen at cup semi-finals and finals. By the early 1990s even the official club souvenir shops were selling replicas of Arab keffiyehs in tangerine and black. By that time the term 'Arabs' had become more widely used, largely as the result of regular references to it by the popular United fanzine the Final Hurdle, which first appeared in 1988."

"Do you know why the word 'nil' is used to mean 'no goals scored' in English football scores?"

A glance at the *Oxford English Dictionary* reveals that the word in the English language is simply a contraction of the Latin word *nihil*, meaning nothing. It has been used in this form since at least 1550, but the first example of it being used in a footballing context doesn't come until March 7 1919, when it shows up in an Oxford University student magazine. "Will some one [sic] remove the jinx?" asks the author as he laments his college's recent on-pitch struggles. "On Friday February 28, we lost to Oriel and Merton by 3 goals to nil."

"I seem to remember hearing Nobel Prize winner Niels Bohr was capped for Denmark. Is this true, and have any other Nobel winners played for their countries?"

A famous Danish physicist whose studies into quantum mechanics and atomic structure won him the Nobel Prize in 1922, Niels Bohr was also a keen goalkeeper for the Danish club Akademisk Boldklub (AB) earlier in the

20th century. As the website of the Danish embassy in Washington explains, "The father, Christian Bohr, had been one of the founders of the [AB] club that took part in introducing football into Denmark and was for a long time the leading club for this sport ... and both Niels Bohr and his slightly younger brother Harald became known as football players before they won fame as scientists. Harald was on the All-Denmark team that won silver at the Olympic Games in London in 1908. Niels did not reach this far, but he was goalkeeper for his club in some of its important matches."

Fellow Nobel winner, Albert Camus, was also a goalkeeper for the University of Algiers, but, contrary to popular belief, never represented Algeria after contracting tuberculosis in 1930, which put an end to his on-field career. At least he found the missing link between football and existentialism. "All I know most surely about morality and obligations, I owe to football," he once said.

"Having read about Tomas Brolin's music video with Dr Alban, I then heard from a friend that Blackburn striker Roque Santa Cruz also sang on a German pop record. This can't be true ... can it?"

Not only did German newspaper Die Welt nominate Roque Santa Cruz as the sexiest footballer of the 2006 World Cup, but he can also boast a top-40 record in both Germany and Austria. In tandem with German "rockers" Sportfreunde Stiller, the Paraguayan sang the title lyrics "Ich, Roque" (I, Roque, or I rock). Roque on indeed.

Widening our search to find the players that have appeared in music videos, it appears the line between music and football is a little more blurred than one might think. First up is the Manchester United forward Carlos Tevez, who is also the front man in a band called Piola Vago, who play *cumbia villera*, a form of Argentinian shantytown/urban music. "Here it's all hip-hop, all in English, so they don't understand a thing," Tevez told the Times of his old West Ham colleagues. "They want to hear it, they ask me, but I say no to them. If they don't understand, what's the point of making them listen to it?" Interestingly, Piola Vago managed to hit the charts in Argentina with their song Lose Your Control, a jaunty little number which, according to the Sun, has Carlitos "singing about whipping a girl and begging her for sex".

A little less raunchy is the former Derby, West Ham

and Hajduk Split defender Igor Stimac, who cut a record in Croatia as part of the Bohems just prior to the 1998 World Cup. "The country went mad about it," recalled Stimac. "We were the Bohems and the record was called Mary and Katie – it was just picked out of nowhere really. It was only me and a group of friends but the song ended up No 1 for four months! I think the sales were really down to Croatia doing well in the tournament rather than my voice! I sang on the record and played guitar."

The former Argentina goalkeeper Germán Burgos also had a predilection for music. Burgos, nicknamed El Mono (the Monkey), is the lead singer in a band called El Monos Supreme and he told the Sun: "The buzz I am getting from my football is the same as I get when I am on stage singing in front of a huge crowd. I still love my music and my band will become a full-time thing when I retire from football – but the way things are going that could be five or six years away."

Another player with a band to fall back on if his career inexplicably goes down the pan is Blackburn's Morten Gamst Pedersen, who fronts Norwegian boy band the Players, alongside fellow footballers Freddy dos Santos, Raymond Kvisvik, Kristofer Hæstad and Øyvind Svenning. Equally unlikely, but no less inexplicable, was the musical "success" of BMD, the triumvirate of Benni McCarthy, Mario Melchiot and Dean Gorre. "We formed a group that we called BMD (based on all our initials) and started recording the track Midas Touch," said

Melchiot. "It was a rap/R&B record – very swingy, very easy on the ears." Hmm. "It took a couple of months, by which time we were ready to perform in a club called Escape in Amsterdam. We had two girls doing the dance moves for us and it went off really well, and after that we were invited to appear on television, twice on a children's channel and also on a prime-time evening show frequented by stars like Janet Jackson and Diana Ross, so we were in good company!"

More famously, there was Liverpool FC's Anfield Rap ("They don't just play but they can rap as well," lied John Barnes in his electro-rap intro), assorted FA Cup final songs too numerous and poor to mention here, Diamond Lights from Chris Waddle and Glenn Hoddle, plus Waddle and Basile Boli's hidden gem We've Got A Feeling. While the evidence is there for all to see on YouTube, German website *www.fc45.de* also provides a detailed list of other footballer aberratio ... sorry, albums. Here you'll find Kevin Keegan's (awful) albums Head Over Heels In Love (Move On Down), England (Somebody Needs) and It Ain't Easy (Do I Know You). Then there is Franz Beckenbauer's Oktoberfest favourite Gute Freunde Kann Niemand Trennen (roughly translated as "you can't separate best friends"), plus I I Am Am Jay Jay, by Jay Jay Okocha, Toni Polster & Die Fabulösen Thekenschlampen's Toni Lass Es Polstern, and Gerd Müller's Dann Macht Es Bumm ("then it goes boom"). Phew!

"Olympos Xylofagou's striker, Panagiotis Pontikos, banged in 16 goals against SEK Ayios Athanasios FC in 2007. Surely this is a record?"

Our friends at the *Guinness Book of Records* can confirm that Pontikos' feat is indeed a record, although one other man has equalled his heroics. Step forward Stephan Stanis, who also scored 16 goals for his side Racing Club in a French Cup match against Aubry Asturies in December 1942.

When it comes to international football, the record number of goals scored by a single player in one match is held by the Australian Archie Thompson, who scored 13 for the Socceroos in their 31-0 World Cup qualifying destruction of American Samoa in 2001. Nineteen of the minnows' 20-man squad had been declared ineligible to play by Fifa, so coach Tunoa Lui was forced to name youth players, including the aptly named 15-year-old Baby Mulipola. "We are going to ask for help from above," said Lui before the game. "We are asking the Lord to help keep the score down." Assistance was not forthcoming as Thompson and his team-mates tore into the youngsters, breaking the previous international football record win of 22-0, which they had set against Tonga barely a week earlier. "They only needed to ensure victory; they did not need to humiliate us," sniffed Lui later.

In England, Luton Town's Joe Payne holds the record for the most goals scored in a league game by an individual player. Payne, who started life on the wing and was playing up front for the first time for the Hatters, scored 10 goals in the 12-0 victory over Bristol Rovers on Easter Monday in 1936.

"My brother met David Mail, one of our Hull City heroes. He'd recently retired from football, was now a lorry driver and confessed that he didn't really like football. Has anyone else heard of any other footballers who don't really like football?"

There are plenty, such as the former Tottenham and Watford goalkeeper Espen Baardsen. He became disillusioned with the game at 25, gave it up and completed an Open University degree, before becoming a financial analyst for London-based hedge fund Eclectica. "It is a great myth that football is easy," he insisted. "It's quite miserable compared to what I have now." Footballer-turned-boxer Curtis Woodhouse is another who disliked the game. "Everyone loves football, but I didn't. It felt like a job," he said. "I felt empty playing, it got me angry. I could have carried on playing football until I was 35, making a nice wage and having a nice life, but that's not what I wanted to do."

Pat Nevin's collaboration with psychologist George Sik for the book, *In Ma Head, Son!* also reveals a fascinating insight into footballers' mentality, as the Scot declares that "being a footballer is what I do. It isn't what I am. I'd always known I was different from other players." The Tottenham defender Benoît Assou-Ekotto shares this laissez-faire attitude to the game. "I don't watch football," he told Sky Sports. "Well, I play it enough, don't I? I don't talk about football away from the game either. I suppose that is unusual. My interests are my friends and music, especially hip-hop. I like Ice Cube and 50 Cent." And a Sunday Mirror report from 2007 also revealed that David Batty, the former England and Leeds midfielder, had especial disdain for internationals. "The national game is boring. And I've not been to watch any match since I finished playing," he said. "I can never understand anybody paying to watch it, never mind going all the way across the world to see it. You want to be entertained."

And so the indifference goes on. Alessandro Rialti, who helped Gabriel Batistuta with his autobiography, explained to the Sunday Times why Batigol never loved the game. "He is not like other players," admitted Rialti. "He is a very good professional who doesn't really like football. Once he leaves the stadium, he doesn't want football encroaching upon the rest of his life. When we were doing the book, he came to my office and for five full days he spoke about his family and his life in Argentina. But when it came to football and his career, he switched off. 'The records are there,' he said. 'You can look them up.'"

"I noticed from reading a list of Celtic's 'other' honours that they have won a surprising number of bizarre trophies. Their list of successes includes such magnificent cups as the Polar Bear Trophy and the Real Madrid Silver Cabin. What's the deal with all these?"

The Bhoys' Polar Bear Trophy triumph came in the 1975 Cup Winners' Cup first-round win over Iceland's FC Valur, who marked their 9-0 aggregate defeat by giving Celtic a stone-carved trophy in the shape of a polar bear devouring a seal. The Real Madrid Silver Cabin, according to Wikipedia, "consists of a silver cabin with a cross on one end of the roof mounted on four silver legs on a marble base", and was given to Celtic by the Spaniards to mark their European Cup quarter-final meeting in 1980, which Real won 3-2 on aggregate. A little less bizarre was their success in the Victory In Europe Cup, a one-off competition played for charity on May 9 1945 to commemorate the end of hostilities in mainland Europe. Rangers turned down the chance to participate because of an upcoming Cup tie, so Queen's Park stepped in at the 11th hour, only to lose out on a corner count-back after the game had finished all square.

But the list of strange trophies doesn't end there. Celtic also won the Empire Exhibition Trophy in 1938, the Saint Mungo Cup in 1951, the 1953 Coronation Cup, the

Alfredo di Stefano Trophy in 1967, the Tolkien-sounding Statuette of Samothrace for being L'Equipe's European team of the year in 1970, plus the 1974 Drybrough Cup. And they also won the 1914 Ferencváros Vase for beating Burnley on a European tour in Budapest, although Celtic didn't receive a trophy for another 74 years after the original one was sold in Hungary to raise funds for the war. Eventually, in Celtic's centenary year, Ferencváros brought "a decorative white porcelain vase, fashioned in the traditional shape of a football cup" to Glasgow.

It's probably also worth mentioning that the Bhoys actually won the quintuple in 1967: in addition to claiming the European Cup, the domestic league title, the Scottish Cup and the Scottish League Cup, they also won the arguably more prestigious Glasgow Cup.

"It is often said that 'Queen of the South' is the only team mentioned in the Bible – but I can find many mentions of 'Bury' (starting in Genesis 23) and 'Reading' (Acts 8:28), and, stretching a point, 'Hearts' and 'Wolves' also get some space. Are there any others I've missed out?"

There are biblical references aplenty, so best to get the most tenuous ones out of the way first. Psalm 80:13 mentions "boars from the *forest* ravage it and the creatures of the field feed on it", while Genesis 12:15

notes, "And when Pharaoh's officials saw her, they praised her to Pharaoh, and she was taken into his *palace*." Isaiah 41:7 even manages to (sort of) cover two Premier League clubs: "The craftsman encourages the goldsmith, and he who smooths with the *hammer spurs* on him who strikes the anvil."

But we can do better. "The Lord has opened his *arsenal* and brought out the weapons of his wrath, for the Sovereign Lord Almighty has work to do in the land of the Babylonians," reads Jeremiah 50:25. There are also the three mentions of Bolivian club the Strongest, in Samuel 11:16, Chronicles 5:2, and Daniel 3:20, while Brazilian outfit Corinthians even share their name with two books in the bible. Our favourite, however, must be this, somewhat dubious, entry in Proverbs 13:23: "A poor *man's field* may produce abundant food, but injustice sweeps it away." Something Stags fans will probably get quicker than most.

"A few years ago in the Premiership, a referee pumped his fist with an exclamation of 'yes!' when a player scored a goal in a certain game. So who was the ref?"

The nugget in question was Mike Reed, who knocked seven bells out of fresh air when Patrik Berger put Liverpool ahead against Leeds during their 3-1 win in

February 2000. Reed claimed he was made up with his own performance, having waved play on after Vladimir Smicer was fouled in the build-up, but the FA was not particularly enamoured with his public display of self-loving. "Having considered the available information, we have issued a reprimand and a warning to Mike Reed," warbled a spokesman. "While we understand the emotions involved, it is essential that match officials do not make gestures which could lead to misinterpretation. The impartiality of our officials must not be open to question. Mr Reed has been warned to keep his emotions under control in future or face further action." He did, but not for long: it was Reed's last season as a professional referee.

"Is it true that Chilean players drank vodka during the 1962 World Cup because they thought it would help their chances of beating the USSR?"

During the group stage, the hosts employed an interesting new tactic of pre-game stereotypical eating: before the opening 3-1 win over Switzerland, they ate cheese, followed by a preparatory meal of spaghetti before the 2-0 success against Italy. Once in the quarter-finals, the Chileans prepared for the USSR clash by downing a couple of Smirnoffs. The ploy actually worked and Chile went on to win 2-1. Coffee was the order of the day before the semi-final with Brazil, but although it perked them up no end in the morning, it couldn't stop the Brazilians winning 4-2 and going on to lift the trophy. Eduardo Galeano later wrote in his book, *Soccer in Sun and Shadow*, that Chile "gobbled down spaghetti, chocolate, and vodka, but choked on the coffee".

"When I was at school in the early 80s, I remember our teacher reading us a novel about a future World Cup in which the finalists were Zaire and Iceland. I seem to remember Iceland winning after nobbling Zaire's Pele-like talisman, who played in bare feet. Have I completely imagined this, or does anyone else recall the book?"

The Ice Warrior, from Robin Chambers' *The Ice Warrior and Other Stories* (published in 1976 by Viking Children's Books), tells how Zaire's star player is killed in a bizarre freezer-related accident. The all-conquering, efficient Iceland (a case of taking symbolism too literally) meet bare-footed and mercurial Zaire in the World Cup final – and the evil Iceland manager plots the downfall of Zaire's star player, Odiwule, who can, apparently, bend the ball 90 degrees. When Zaire are awarded a free-kick, Iceland's equivalent of Douglas Jardine swaps the ball with a special refrigerated one he had been keeping under the team bench (how he did this without anyone else seeing in unclear).

When the Zairean maestro strikes the ball, his foot and leg shatter (it's those modern boots, you know) and he is killed instantly. The chilly northern cheats win the final. Fast forward 10 years and a vengeful ghost of the victim returns to haunt the Iceland manager, who has, rather unusually, become the country's prime minister.

"We've all heard of youngsters who grew up in slums to become professional footballers, but what is the greatest rags-to-riches story of them all?"

It's a subjective matter, of course, but you could do worse than start with one of the world's greatest ever players, Diego Maradona. Before becoming a legend, Diego grew up in the shanty town of Villa Fiorito, where he shared one room with seven siblings. Sanitation facilities were somewhat crude and one night, when still a toddler, Maradona fell into the family cesspit after losing his way in the dark. Fortunately his Uncle Cirilo, screaming, "Diegito, keep your head above the shit", was on hand to rescue the youngster. "It wasn't easy, eh? Nothing was easy," recalled Maradona with masterful understatement. One local resident remembered El Diego's formative years thus: "He had nothing else but football," said Jose Trotte. "He was not educated, he had no sophistication. He was shirtless and barefooted. He was just this street kid with a gift from God." The rest, as they say, is history.

Brazil also offers plenty of rags-to-riches tales. The 1999 European Footballer of the Year, Rivaldo, was so impoverished as a child that he lost his teeth to malnutrition and was dangerously thin and muscularly underdeveloped right into his teens. Then there is the three-times Fifa World Player of the Year, Ronaldo, whose first chance to escape the poverty-stricken streets of Rio evaporated when he couldn't raise the bus fare to attend a trial with Flamengo. His former Real Madrid team-mate Roberto Carlos also grew up in conditions far from the luxury he now basks in. According to John Carlin in an Observer article from 2002, the free-shooting left-back developed his inordinately thick thighs by "working as a sort of human ox, spending hour after hour in the fields alongside his father pushing or pulling outrageously heavy pieces of farm machinery".

It is also worth mentioning the former Newcastle and Portsmouth forward Lomana LuaLua, who arrived in Britain with his father at the age of nine as an asylum seeker from the Democratic Republic of Congo (then Zaire). The France midfielder Rio Mavuba is another former asylum seeker who became a professional footballer. His father, Mafuila Mavuba, was part of the Zaire squad at the 1974 World Cup and later went to live in Angola, where he disappeared during the civil war and was presumed killed. After his mother fled, Rio was born on a refugee boat off the coast of West Africa en route to France.

The former Arsenal and Portsmouth full-back Lauren is another who had a narrow escape. His father, Valentin Bisan-Etame, was a prominent politician in Equatorial Guinea during the reign (1968-79) of psychotic dictator Francisco Macias Nguema. In 1977, Valentin took the noble but potentially fatal decision to oppose Nguema's widespread killings and theft, and was imprisoned and sentenced to death. An uncle in the army helped Valentin, several of his kids and his heavily pregnant wife escape to Cameroon, where Lauren was born. "If our family hadn't escaped, I probably wouldn't have been born," surmised Lauren. "We lived in Cameroon until I was three years old, and after that we went to Spain, because Guinea was a Spanish colony." He grew up in Montequinto, a rough part of Seville, with his parents and 14 brothers.

Collins John's early life was no easier. His father was murdered by guerrillas in Liberia in 1991, when he was just six. John, his mother and younger brothers lived in constant fear that they would suffer the same fate. They were also desperately poor. "I had nothing more than a pair of underpants," the Fulham forward recalled. "We didn't have food every day. It was a real struggle because of the civil war." The family escaped Liberia two years later and, after living in a Rotterdam refugee camp for a further two years, were eventually given Dutch citizenship. Before making his Fulham debut, John told Dutch journalists how he planned to celebrate his first goal. "I think I'll run all around the pitch and reveal the words I will have written in black letters on a white vest underneath my shirt," he said. "It will read: 'For my past'. I'll do it for everything I have gone through, for all the suffering. But most of all I will do it for my dad."

Finally, for rags-to-riches-and-back-to-rags stories, it's hard to beat that of the late Brazilian legend Garrincha, or Manuel Francisco dos Santos, as he was born in Pau Grande, a British-owned town near Rio. Residents were effectively the subjects of a British trading company who clothed, housed and controlled every facet of their lives. Garrincha began working in the local factory when he was 14, but football was to provide a way out for him – even though he had bow-shaped legs of unequal length. In his Guardian review of Ruy Castro's biography, *Triumph and Tragedy of Brazil's Forgotten Footballing Hero*, Josh Lacey offered the following synopsis of Garrincha's life after that: "He lost his virginity to a goat, slept with hundreds of women and sired at least 14 children. When he played for the Brazilian national team in the 1950s and early 60s, he scored 34 goals and won the World Cup twice. He killed his mother-in-law in a car crash, then died of drink [aged 49, in 1983]."

"A friend of mine bullishly claimed he'd heard that a match was once postponed on almost 30 separate occasions. Is he having me on?"

Hail your friend, for he speaks the truth. Back in the icy winter of 1979, the Scottish Cup second-round clash between Inverness Thistle and Falkirk had to be postponed no fewer than 29 times. The original date for the game was January 6, but the clubs had to wait 47 days until the Kingsmills Park ground was eventually declared playable, on February 22. When the match finally took place, four first-half goals helped Falkirk seal their spot in the third round. However, because of the 71-day period between the second-round draw and Falkirk's win, Billy Little's side were forced to visit Dundee just three days later in round three, where a late penalty ended their cup journey.

Remarkably, the tie is still eclipsed by another Scottish Cup game that took place 16 years earlier, when sub-zero conditions again played havoc with the fixture list, not just in Scotland but all across Britain. More than 400 English league and cup matches fell victim to the weather and the season had to be extended by a month on both sides of the border. While one FA Cup third-round tie between Coventry and Lincoln eventually took place at the 16th time of asking, the clash between Airdrie and Stranraer was busy setting a British record of 33 postponements. For

Airdrie it was 34th time lucky as they ran out 3-0 victors.

Incidentally, the worst day of domestic cancellations did not occur in 1962-63. That honour went to February 3 1940, when just one of 56 wartime league matches beat the weather. Plymouth made the most of their moment in the limelight with a 10-3 thumping of Bristol City.

"Was Joey Barton the first player to be punished by the FA for mooning at Everton in 2007?"

No, is the brief answer. In the 1970s, Terry Mancini (of QPR) and Sammy Nelson (of Arsenal) were both suspended for buttock-baring. Mancini, in the middle of a dispute regarding a possible transfer to Arsenal, gave the directors' box an eyeful of 'arris after one match at Loftus Road. The referee turned a blind eye to Mancini's, er, blind eye, but the incident was publicised on Match of the Day; as a result, Mancini was banned for two matches and fined £150. It sort of served its purpose, though: four days after baring his backside, Mancini got his move to Highbury. Where he would meet Sammy Nelson, who himself mooned to the North Bank to celebrate scoring at both ends in a 1-1 draw with Coventry in 1979. He was banned for two weeks.

That was that until 1988, when Wimbledon's Crazy Gang – led inevitably by that overzealous thespian

Vincent Jones – celebrated Alan Cork's testimonial by standing on the halfway line and revealing *their* halfway lines to the whole of Plough Lane. Nine players had to pay £750 apiece to the FA for their art, with the club fined £5,000 for failing to control their players' pants. "It was Alan Cork's testimonial on the Monday night and we had won the FA Cup final on the previous Saturday," remembered John Scales, one of the Wimbledon Nine. "We were sponsored by Carlsberg at the time so we got cans of Carlsberg coming out of everywhere. The partying had just gone on and it was in its third stage by that day; we were egged on by the supporters and we were easy bait."

"Francis Jeffers has played one senior game for England, in which he scored a goal against Australia. Does this make Franny the most prolific goalscorer in international football?"

Jeffers may have a goals-per-international ratio of 1.00, but this one-game statistic still leaves him well adrift of the most prolific international strikers the game has known. Thankfully. In terms of England players with greater records (and we'll use 20 caps as a minimum throughout), we can start with Steve Bloomer (1874-1938), the former Derby striker, cricketer, baseball star and all-round celebrity of his day. In 23 internationals,

Bloomer scored 28 times, a ratio of 1.22 goals per game. Overlapping Bloomer's England career was that of Viv Woodward, who represented his country between 1903 and 1911, scoring 29 times in 23 internationals (1.26). And though George Camsell didn't make 20 caps, he's still worthy of a mention for his record of 18 goals in nine memorable internationals.

As far as other international players' record ratios are concerned, there was Hungary's Sándor Kocsis, who racked up 75 goals in an eight-year career comprising 68 internationals (1.10). Sharing that ratio from his 62 caps for West Germany is Gerd Müller, who scored 68 times, while Sweden's Sven Rydell banged in 49 goals in just 43 games (1.14). Even further in front, however, are two fellow Scandinavians: his compatriot Gunnar Nordahl's 1.30 ratio came courtesy of his 43 international strikes from 33 games, while Denmark's Poul "Tist" Nielsen performed even better. In a career spanning more than 15 years, but just 38 caps, Nielsen scored 52 times – a ratio of 1.37 goals for every international he played.

"Is Juventus' attendance of 237 against Sampdoria in the 2005-06 Coppa Italia a record low for any top-flight team in the big European leagues (barring games played behind closed doors, of course)?"

We haven't been able to find anything more miserable than that, but were amused to find that Europe's least appealing club competition may well be the InterToto Cup. The 2003 first-round clash between Olympiakos Nicosia and ZTS Dubnica (Slovakia) attracted an impressive 71 punters, while a far more respectable 80 turned up two years later as Olympiakos Nicosia hosted Gloria Bistrita (Romania), again in the first round. On the international front, the record low for Uefa competitions remains the Euro 1996 qualifier between Azerbaijan and Poland in Trabzon (Turkey), when precisely 200 hardy souls went out of their way to watch a 0-0 draw.

"Zambian Laughter Chilembe has played in Zimbabwe for Caps United FC, while I also know about Surprise Moriri from Mamelodi Sundowns in South Africa. But my favourite is one called Have-A-Look Dube playing for Njube Sundowns here in Zimbabwe! Any more strange/funny/good/ridiculous football names anyone can dredge up?"

Givemore Manuella, Gift Makolonio and Method Mwanyazi of Caps United in Zimbabwe are great names, but they pale into comparison beside Limited Chicafa and the outstandingly named Danger Fourpence. There's also Stephen Sunny Sunday, who plays for Polideportivo Ejido in Spain, plus South Africa's Naughty Makoena and Tonic Chabalala. Austrian side SC Schwanenstadt also boast midfielder Osa Guobadia, who has the name Ice Cream on the back of his shirt.

Brazilian forward Creedence Clearwater Couto obviously had parents who were big fans of the American songsters, while notable mentions also go to the former England internationals Harry Daft and Segar Bastard (who, incidentally, refereed an FA Cup final, played cricket for Essex and owned a racehorse). However, it would be foolish of us to ignore Anthony Philip David Terry Frank Donald Stanley Gerry Gordon Stephen James Oatway – Charlie to his friends ("I'm named after the QPR 1972-73 promotion-winning team," explained the long-time Brighton player) – or three of our favourites: Australian keeper Norman Conquest, Seychelles star Johnny Moustache and Congolese striker Bongo Christ.

Last but not least, Florian Kinast, the sports editor of German newspaper Abendzeitung, dropped us a line from Munich. "I remember Franco Foda, a three-time German Cup winner with Kaiserslautern, Leverkusen and Stuttgart between 1990 and 1997 and then head coach of Austrian team SK Sturm Graz," he explained. "Despite his success elsewhere he only played twice for Germany, making his debut away to Brazil in December 1987. Obviously this would usually be a great honour, but not so much in Foda's case. He came on as a substitute with eight minutes to go, emerging to howls of laughter from the stands as his name went up on the scoreboard. *Franco foda*, sadly, means 'fucking for free' in Portuguese. Brazil's players may have been distracted a bit, too: Stefan Reuter snatched an equaliser in the 90th minute."

"Do you know which football club opened its ground for ice-skating because the pitch was frozen?"

The year was 1962-63, and England and Wales were experiencing their coldest winter since 1740 (Scotland, incidentally, was suffering its worst since 1829). From Boxing Day 1962 to early March 1963, most of the British Isles was under snow, with temperatures five to seven degrees below average. Not surprisingly, hardly any football was played. Indeed, the winter was so severe that Barnsley only managed two games from December 21 1962 to March 12 1963. Up the road in Halifax, however, they hit upon an enterprising idea: why not use the Shay for ice-skating?

Ironically, it happened on March 2 1963, when – as the Manchester Guardian booklet The Long Winter 1962-63 reports – most of the country was, at long last, experiencing a thaw. "Troops relieved a farm on Dartmoor which had been cut off by 20ft snow drifts for 66 days. With only 14 Football League matches postponed, soccer had its best day for 11 weeks. There was still no football at Halifax, but the local club opened its ground as a public ice rink and hundreds skated on it." The stunt pulled in a few pennies, but it didn't do Halifax any good – they scraped just 30 points all season and were relegated to the Fourth Division.

"My dorm mate broached the sensitive topic of the Blue Peter Garden trashing of 1983, which may or may not have involved Les Ferdinand. After a thorough search of the web, I found little information relating to the event and would like to ask you for clarification, as to the extent of his involvement in the horrible trashing."

Nothing is 100% clear, even now, more than 25 years after that terrible day. Former presenter Mark Curry, in a moment away from his X-Files collection, suggested that the government had broken in to dig up the time capsule buried by Peter Purves and chums because it contained information about UFOs. We don't know too much about that, but we have established that, talking to the BBC Choice programme, 45 Minutes, Sir Les denied it had been his size eights trampling on Janet Ellis's beloved hyacinths, but admitted that he had "helped a few people over the wall". At the time, Percy Thrower comforted Janet with the knowledge that whoever had done it "must be mentally ill".

However, when we finally confronted Ferdinand in 2007, he'd changed his tune. "Now *that* was a joke!" he claimed. "What happened was I was on a programme and for some reason they got to talking about the vandalism of the Blue Peter garden and they said: 'You grew up and went to school around that area, were you involved?' I just said something like 'No, there were bigger and badder boys than me around', but they kept on asking me; apparently they were convinced that me and Dennis Wise had done it. So eventually, because it seemed like it was obviously a light-hearted conversation, I jokingly said, 'Yeah, we helped those guys over the wall.' The next day I woke up and there was a tabloid journalist at my door showing me pictures of Percy Thrower crying and telling me they were going to run my admission on their front page! ["Blue Peter garden was trashed by soccer star Ferdinand's gang," ran the Sun's headline.] I kept telling them it was a just a joke but they were having none of it. It was ridiculous!"

"I vaguely remember waking up on Boxing Day morning a couple of years ago (with a massive hangover) and seeing a caption on Football Focus with an old list of Boxing Day fixtures and an awful lot of goals. Was it something to do with the DTs or did this really happen?"

On December 26 1963, an amazing 66 goals were scored in the old First Division, leaving some teams wishing there had been a repeat of the previous season's Big Freeze. Here are the classifieds:

Blackpool 1-5 Chelsea, Burnley 6-1 Man Utd, Fulham 10-1 Ipswich, Leicester 2-0 Everton, Liverpool 6-1 Stoke, Nottingham Forest 3-3 Sheffield United, West Brom 4-4

Tottenham, Sheffield Wednesday 3-0 Bolton, Wolves 3-3 Aston Villa, West Ham 2-8 Blackburn.

If that wasn't weird enough, the results two days later – when many of the teams played the "return leg" – beggar belief. West Ham, who had lost 8-2 at home to Blackburn, won 3-1 at Ewood Park. Manchester United, fresh from a 6-1 thrashing at Burnley, turned the tables at Old Trafford with a 5-1 win. And poor Ipswich, who had clearly been on the Christmas Day pop, avenged their 10-1 defeat by Fulham with a 4-2 victory over the Cottagers at Portman Road. Much good the two points did them, mind you: they finished bottom.

"I set the questions for the weekly pub quiz and asked the following question: the 1986 Mexico World Cup was originally meant to be held in which South American country? Let me know your answer as mine was challenged by the rest of the pub!"

In 1974 Fifa awarded the 1986 World Cup to Colombia – but infrastructure and financial problems meant that by 1983 the country was struggling to meet its promises. Realising the prospects of a World Cup in Colombia were slim, Brazil, Canada, Mexico and the United States offered themselves as alternatives for the tournament. After Colombia were forced to drop out, Brazil decided they weren't interested in World Cup 86 after all. And so Fifa, faced with three competing bids, decided in May 1983 to reject Canada and the US in favour of Mexico.

There was much outrage in the USA about the decision. Henry Kissinger, the leader of the US bid, even petitioned Fifa for another chance, arguing that the 1986 tournament would revive the fading North American Soccer League (NASL). He was supported by Pele and Franz Beckenbauer – but Fifa's president, João Havelange, was singularly unimpressed. Fifa claimed its decision was down to logistics – the US bid included venues on the east and west coast, which meant increased travelling times and weary footballers. But the real reason was that it wanted to teach US football a lesson.

In 1981, Fifa had threatened to outlaw the NASL and suspend the US Federation because the NASL had changed the offside line from halfway to 35 yards out and used a shoot-out to decide drawn matches. The NASL refused to back down – and even threatened legal action against Fifa. But what goes around comes around, and two years later Fifa got its revenge by rejecting Kissinger's bid. With the last hope of reviving the NASL gone, it folded before the start of the 1986 World Cup. "It makes me nostalgic for the Middle East," said the former secretary of state, referring to his dealings with Fifa.

"Would you know the title and artist on the Champions League football theme tune? I've tried everywhere with no results. I would love to buy a copy."

Why, yes. The Guardian's very own Notes and Queries had pretty much the definitive answer, courtesy of Judith Colman from Edinburgh. "The music is a bowdlerisation of Handel's coronation anthem, Zadok the Priest," she said, which we presume is a bad thing. "As a member of the choir singing on the recording, I am ashamed to say I can still remember the words: 'We are the champions; wir sind die Besten; nous sommes les meilleurs.'" As Uefa's Helen Wood added, "British composer, Tony Britten, was commissioned to write and arrange the music in a Handelian style in 1992. The song was called Champions League."

The anthem was performed by the Royal Philarmonic Orchestra and sung by the Academy of St Martin in the Fields Chorus. However, here's the heartbreaker: the music has still not been commercialised and it is therefore not possible to buy it in any shops. Still, if you follow Judith's advice, maybe you could go for a take on the original and just add your own vocals.

"I seem to remember my father telling me that a football match in South America once kick-started a war. Is this true, and if so, how did it happen?"

It's almost true. "The 'Football War" was fought by Central American countries El Salvador and Honduras in 1969. In fact, it also went by the name of the "100 Hours' War", and in reality there were a host of issues at the root of the troubles. Migration, trade and simmering land disputes on the border all conspired to spark social unrest between the two, but it wasn't until the best-of-three World Cup qualifiers in 1969 that the tipping point was reached.

The first game – a 1-0 win for Honduras – in Tegucigalpa witnessed disturbances but things deteriorated significantly come the second in San Salvador: visiting Honduran players, according to Ryszard Kapuściński's 1978 book *Wojna Futbolowa*, endured a sleepless night before the game, with rotten eggs, dead rats and stinking rags all tossed through the broken windows of their hotel; Honduran fans were brutalised at the game, and the country's flag and national anthem were also mocked. "Under such conditions the players from Tegucigalpa did not, understandably, have their minds on the game," admitted the Honduras coach Mario Griffin after his team lost 3-0. "They had their minds on getting out alive. We're awfully lucky that we lost."

Tensions continued to increase before the decisive third match in Mexico, with the press stoking the frenzy. And on June 27 – the day of the play-off – Honduras broke off diplomatic relations with their neighbour. El Salvador eventually triumphed 3-2 after extra-time, booking their place in the 1970 World Cup (where they would lose all three of their group games without scoring). By July 14, El Salvador had invaded Honduras. When the Organisation of American States negotiated a ceasefire on July 20, approximately 1,000 to 2,000 people had lost their lives and 100,000 more had become refugees. Troops from El Salvador were withdrawn in August, but it wasn't until 11 years later that a peace treaty between the nations was agreed. A civil war in El Salvador ensued between 1980 until 1992, when the International Court of Justice awarded much of the originally disputed territory to Honduras.

It is also arguable that the disintegration of Yugoslavia can be traced back to a game of football: Red Star Belgrade's trip to Dinamo Zagreb on May 13 1990. It was a taut period in Yugoslavia, with communism losing its grip and politicians in Croatia and Slovenia increasingly calling for looser ties with the other republics in the federation (Bosnia and Herzegovina, Macedonia, Montenegro and Serbia). Serbia, led by Slobodan Milosevic, opposed such a move, but just five days before the match, the Franjo Tudjman-led Croatian Democratic Union (HDZ) – whose main campaign platform had been independence for Croatia – won the first free, multiparty, elections in the republic for 50 years, heightening the sense of tension.

Several thousand Red Star fans, including a hooligan group called Delije (Tough Guys) – led by Serbian nationalist Zeljko Raznatovi (also known, rather more infamously, as Arkan) – made the journey to Zagreb, and fights between rival fans started outside the stadium long before kick-off. When the match started, the Delije tore up seats and attacked peaceful sections of the home support. In response, Dinamo's own hooligans buckled a massive fence penning them in and stormed the pitch in an attempt to confront Red Star's fans. It took 70 minutes to subdue the ensuing riots, and while Red Star's players beat a retreat, a number of Dinamo players joined in the fighting, most notably Zvonamir Boban, who famously delivered a flying kick to a policeman he saw attacking a Dinamo fan.

Croatia's subsequent war of independence didn't truly get going until the following year – after Croatia first declared its independence from Yugoslavia in June – but, as American journalist Franklin Foer points out in his book, *How Soccer Explains the World: An Unlikely Theory of Globalization*, this was "the first time in 50 years that Yugoslavia had seen its ethnic groups openly battle one another". Over the next year a series of further minor skirmishes between Croatian authorities and Serbians living within Croatia took place, and while football certainly didn't provide the cause for the resulting civil war, many people do still hold the riot at the Maksimir as its first battle. The Zagreb newspaper, Vecernji List, observed in 2005 that "the game that was never played will be remembered, at least by the soccer fans, as the beginning of the Patriotic War, and almost all of the contemporaries will declare it the key in understanding the Croatian cause".

On a happier note, football once stopped a war – albeit temporarily. The opposing sides in Nigeria's Biafran war declared a brief truce so that they could watch Pele and his touring Santos team play in two exhibition matches.

"A bad result can precipitate a firing – but has there ever been a manager sacked during a game?"

We thought the nearest instance was that of the former Wales boss Bobby Gould, who once resigned as Peterborough's coach during half-time. During the interval of Posh's LDV Vans tie at Bristol City in September 2004, with the score 1-0 to the hosts, Gould decided he had seen enough. "At half-time we said a few things and Bob never contributed anything," explained then-manager Barry Fry. "As I was going out for the second half Bob said, 'That is me, I'm packing up, I can't be associated with that side.'" Gould's dramatic decision had little effect on the team, who still lost 1-0.

However, we then stumbled upon the case of Don Mackay, formerly the manager of Coventry and Blackburn, who was two years into his spell in charge of Fulham when he was forced out of the club – during a match at Leyton Orient in 1994. A common misconception is that chairman Jimmy Hill stormed into the dressing room and sacked Mackay, although the Scot has since revealed exactly what happened. "He [Hill] didn't have the bottle to sack me, so he sent his vice-chairman around instead."

One man who did have the guts to wield the axe mid-game was the Fortuna Cologne club president Jean Loering, with former Germany goalkeeper and one-man-Patrick-Battiston-destroyer Harald Schumacher on the receiving end. In charge of Second Division side Fortuna Cologne in 1999, Schumacher received his long-overdue marching orders while giving a half-time team talk.

With his side trailing 2-0 to Waldhof Mannheim, Loering popped into the dressing room and told Schumacher to leave there and then. "I asked Toni [sic] not to come back for the second half. I wanted him to leave the stadium immediately. I had hesitated from firing him for quite a long time – but I had to do it then," said Loering. "He is arrogant and selfish. He always thinks he's the only one who knows anything about football. But with regard to his tactics, he did not know whether he was a man or a woman. One minute we were all defence, the next we were all attack. It was not just the fans who were confused, but the players as well. I idolised Schumacher as a player but I am not going to sit on my hands while he takes my club to the grave." Schumacher stormed out of the ground, leaving assistant Ralf Minge in charge, but the extreme measure made little short-term difference: Fortuna still lost the game 5-1.

"Is it true that Morrissey is mates with the former QPR striker Kevin Gallen?"

Rather randomly, the Mancunian miserablist *is* an acquaintance of Gallen. According to an article in the League Paper, Morrissey met Gallen in Los Angeles in June 2005 – he was recording album Ringleader of the Tormentors, while the striker was in the city on holiday. Subsequently the pair became "email friends"; Gallen even sent Morrissey a personalised kit with "Mozalini 10" on the back. "I've invited him to see a game when he's next back in England," said Gallen, himself the one-time owner of Rangers' No10 shirt.

"What is the first recorded incident of football violence or hooliganism?"

Football and violence go way back – at least seven centuries back, in fact. In 1314, for instance, Edward II banned football (at that stage a nasty free-for-all involving rival villages fly-hacking a pig's bladder across the local heath) because he believed the disorder surrounding matches might lead to social unrest or possibly even treason. As detailed by the Social Issues Research Centre, the mayor of London, Nicholas Farndon said: "And whereas there is a great uproar in the City through certain tumults arising from the striking of great footballs in the field of the public – from which many evils perchance may arise – which may God forbid – we do command and do forbid, on the King's behalf, upon pain of imprisonment, that such games shall not be practised henceforth within this city."

If you're talking about the modern game, then look no further than the 1880s and, in particular, Preston North End. In May 1885, Preston's 5-0 friendly win over Aston Villa sent the fans into a frenzy. "Roughs congregated around the Preston team, [each of whom] came in for [his] share of treatment," explained a report in the Birmingham Gazette. "The Preston men, with commendable courage, turned upon the crowd surrounding them and retaliated. A free fight quickly ensued, during the course of which several aerated water

bottles were hurled into the crowd and smashed, regardless of the consequences." One of the Preston players was beaten so severely that he lost consciousness. The following year Preston fans notched up another first – fighting Queens Park fans in a railway station. Another milestone of sorts was reached in 1905 when several Preston supporters were tried for hooliganism, including a "drunk and disorderly" 70-year-old woman, following their match against Blackburn.

In the inter-war years a brake was applied to such incidents, but in the 1950s – along with the Mods, Rockers and Elvis – came a second wave of hooliganism.

In the 1955-56 season, Liverpool and Everton fans were involved in several train-wrecking incidents and by the 1960s an average of 25 hooligan incidents a year were being reported – and hooliganism as we know it had been born.

"When did the first live televised football match take place in Britain?"

Four years before Kenneth Wolstenholme uttered his first words on Match of the Day, ITV broadcast the first ever live league game on British TV. As detailed in Gary Imlach's book, *My Father and Other Working-Class Football Heroes*, ITV agreed a deal with the Football League to cover 26 league games in the 1960-61 season: "On September 10 1960 Blackpool's home game with Bolton became the first live match on British television. But the first Big Game was a flop. ITV put their cameras high up behind the goal at Bloomfield Road rather than on the halfway line in the main stand. The critics complained that the commentators over-praised what everyone could see was a poor game, and talked about a packed house when the crowd was only 17,000 in a ground that held twice as many." By the time Newcastle travelled to Arsenal for ITV's next feature, the Gunners' board refused entry to the cameras. "The deal collapsed," adds Imlach. "ITV withdrew their offer, and in the fallout from the whole affair the BBC did the same with their proposal to show FA Cup games."

It wasn't as if television companies hadn't covered live football before, though. Twenty-three years earlier, the BBC had televised the 1937 FA Cup final on May 1 between Sunderland and Preston – in part – before an estimated 10,000 audience got to enjoy Preston's return against Huddersfield a year later in its entirety.

Yet historians at Arsenal deliver a conflicting view, claiming it was they who broadcast the first full British game of football. "On September 16 1937, parts of a match between the club's first team and reserves was broadcast live," claims their website. "This was the first time that people from up and down the length of Britain had been able to watch a game of football live."

"While flicking through some stats, I noticed that Alan Shearer scored five hat-tricks for Blackburn in 1995-96. Has any other player scored more in one season?"

First up, the Wolves striker Steve Bull scored six of his 18 career hat-tricks in the 1988-89 season, although two of these were four-goal hauls against Preston and Port Vale. Matching this feat are Jimmy Greaves (for Chelsea in 1960-61), Ayr United's Jimmy Smith (1927-28) and Altrincham's Jackie Swindells, who scored 82 goals in 63 games during the 1965-66 campaign, 18 of which came from six hat-tricks. Of course, when famous goalscoring achievements are mentioned, William Ralph 'Dixie' Dean's name is usually close behind ... as is the case here. Dean scored seven of his record 37 career hat-tricks in 1927-28, but went one better in the 1931-32 season.

Remarkably, even that can't lay claim to the record, which instead belongs to Framwellgate Moor's most famous son. George Camsell, a Middlesbrough legend whose talents were first spotted – according to the Observer's Paul Wilson – at a "pithead kickabout during a miners' strike", banged home nine hat-tricks in the 1925-26 campaign. They helped comprise a season tally of 59 goals from just 37 games, a record that was, in turn, eclipsed by Dean the very next season. Camsell also scored 18 goals for England in just nine appearances, a total that would surely have been greater had Dean and Cliff Bastin not been on the scene at the same time.

"My wife and I have won international caps for the British Virgin Islands women's and men's football teams. Are we the only such couple or are there any instances of other married couples getting international caps?"

Impressive a feat as it is, you aren't the sole members of this exclusive club. For instance, the Portsmouth defender Hermann Hreidarsson and his wife Ragna Lóa Stefánsdóttir – also a centre-back – both own a fancy collection of Icelandic caps. "I know some footballers' wives are not very interested in football, but Ragna is different," he told the Sun. "I don't know any other footballer who married a player!" He didn't look very hard. Haraldur Ingólfsson, formerly with Akranes (and, for a short spell, Aberdeen as well), and his wife Jónína Víglundsdóttir both played for Iceland between 1992 and 1995. Staying in Scandinavia, both Hans Eskilsson and Malin Swedberg played for Sweden. She represented her country 78 times, while he was the less successful in the couple with just eight caps.

Another couple that share a collection of caps as well as a conjugal association are the former United States captain Claudio Reyna and his wife Danielle Egan. And north of the border, the Vancouver Whitecaps' Steve Kindel and Sara Maglio won four and six caps for Canada, respectively, during their careers.

However, the highest-profile, nearest-miss example of an international footballing couple must be Ronaldo and Milene Domingues, who first got together after he spotted her on television. The Brazil striker eventually popped the question, while Milene broke the world keepy-uppy record, gave birth to baby Ronald ("my wife and I eat a lot at McDonald's so we chose Ronald," explained the toothy one) and was selected for Brazil's 2003 women's World Cup campaign. Sadly she never played, the pair divorced and she remains without an international cap to this day.

"What is the greatest top-flight comeback ever?"

There have been a host of teams that have fought back from 3-0 down to draw 3-3 (including Liverpool, against Manchester United in January 1994; and Southampton, against Liverpool in August 2000). However, Wolves have bettered this, recovering from three goals down against Leicester to score four in the final 38 minutes and win 4-3 in November 2003, while Leeds can match this too, having fought back from a similar deficit at home to Derby in November 1997 to win 4-3. However, the greatest Premiership fightback belongs to Manchester United, who, on September 29 2001, gave Spurs a three-goal start at White Hart Lane, before storming back to score five without reply in the second half.

Regarding comebacks in English football BS (before Sky), there was QPR's famous 5-5 draw against Newcastle in September 1984, arguably the greatest game ever witnessed on plastic. QPR trailed 4-0 at half-time, but eventually hauled themselves level at 5-5 courtesy of Gary Micklewhite's last-gasp goal.

But the greatest comeback ever belongs to Charlton, who trailed Huddersfield 5-1 with only half an hour left in their Second Division match on December 21 1957. The scoreline made sense: defensively inept Charlton, who had been relegated the previous season after conceding 120 goals, had been playing with 10 men ever since their captain, Derek Ufton, was stretchered off after 15 minutes with a dislocated shoulder (there were no subs in those days). What followed did not.

Charlton's solitary goal at that point had been scored by Johnny Summers. But then the winger really got to work. He scored a second and, a minute later, set one up for John Ryan: 5-3. By the time the next 10 minutes were up, Summers had scored another three, bringing his personal total to a club-record five. Charlton had amazingly taken a 6-5 lead. Huddersfield did at least rise from their slumber to score an equaliser. But with the last kick of the match, Summers laid on another goal for Ryan and a frankly ridiculous 7-6 victory was complete. No team other than Huddersfield has scored six goals in a league match and still lost. What their manager Bill Shankly said in the dressing room after the game is thankfully not recorded.

"Who was the first black professional footballer?"

According to the author Phil Vasili, the first black professional footballer was Arthur Wharton (1865-1930), who played for Sheffield United, Preston North End and Darlington. Arthur was born to parents who were both mixed race (his father was half Grenadian and half Scottish; his mother was half Scottish and half Fante Royal of the stool family of Ekumfie) and he lived in a Victorian society where cultural Darwinism was rampant.

But Wharton made a mockery of such racial theories. Not only was he the world's first black professional footballer (he was on United's books at the same time as the legendary "Fatty" Foulkes), but he also held the world record for the 100-yard dash and was probably the first African to play professional cricket in Britain. Sadly, Wharton died in poverty and is buried in an unmarked grave in Edlington, near Doncaster. For more information, read Vasili's *The First Black Footballer – Arthur Wharton 1865-1930: An Absence of Memory*.

"Is it true that an FA Cup winner was hanged for sheep stealing in Australia in the early 1900s? I was told that it was an ex-Everton player."

After a prolonged spell of debate, the name of Goodison Park legend Alexander "Sandy" Young popped up. However, according to Bob Goodwin's *Complete Who's Who of Tottenham Hotspur*, the one-time Spurs striker was imprisoned – and not executed – for far more wayward ways.

". . . [Young] had a year with South Liverpool before emigrating to Australia in 1914," wrote Goodwin. "In December 1915, Young was charged with the wilful murder of his brother and, in June 1916, was found guilty of manslaughter, evidence having been produced from football officials in England that during his playing career he had been subject to fits of temporary insanity. He was sentenced to three years' imprisonment but was not released immediately on completion of his sentence but kept in custody on the grounds of 'mental weakness' and it was some time before he returned home to Scotland ..." Young is believed to have died on September 17 1959 in Portobello, Edinburgh.

"It is often claimed that Liverpool were the first British club to have a shirt sponsor (Hitachi in 1979), but while they were doubtless the first professional club to be sponsored, I'm pretty sure Kettering beat them to it by a few years. Maybe you can confirm it?"

Having spoken to Kettering's club historian Mel Hopkins, we can indeed. When the Wolves striker Derek Dougan retired from football in the summer of 1975, he joined Southern League club Kettering Town as chief executive. Within a month of his appointment, he had brokered a "four-figure" deal with local firm Kettering Tyres, and in a SL game against Bath City on January 24 1976, Kettering became the first British club to run out with a company's name emblazoned on their shirts.

Sadly, the groundbreaking new strip would not get another run-out. Four days later, the FA predictably ordered the club to remove the new slogan, despite Dougan's claim that the ruling body's 1972 ban on sponsorship had not been put down in writing.

Characteristically, Dougan didn't take this body blow lying down. He cheekily changed the wording on the shirts to Kettering T, which he claimed stood for Town and had nothing whatsoever to do with Tyres. For a couple of heady months, the team played on under the new slogan. Sure enough, however, Kettering were soon up before the FA, who in April ordered them to "remove the words Kettering T from their strip". The threat of a £1,000 fine was too much for such a small club, and the words were reluctantly removed.

There would be one final irony. Kettering didn't let the matter lie – after all, clubs like Bayern Munich had been coining it in on the continent for years – and so, alongside Derby and Bolton, they put forward a proposal to the FA regarding shirt sponsorship. But although the proposal was accepted on June 3 1977, Kettering could not find a sponsor for the following season.

"Can anyone explain the archaic tactic of 'metodo', beloved of the Austrian side of the 1950s, I believe?"

During football's formative years, attack was the name of the game. The barnstorming 2-3-5 formation was king, while the classic W-M formation – used by England after the war – was merely a glint in Walter Winterbottom's eye. But during the 1930s, Italy's coach Vittorio Pozzo was formulating an idea which was to become known as the Italian *metodo*.

Pozzo decided that 2-3-5 was just a little bit too bold and decided to pull his two inside-forwards back into midfield, making a sort of 2-3-2-3 formation. Five men in midfield obviously worked, as Italy won successive World Cups in 1934 and 1938 and Pozzo was hailed as a tactical genius. Incidentally, before the 1938 World Cup, fascist dictator Benito Mussolini sent a telegram to Pozzo which said "win or die". Fortunately for the creator of *metodo*, Italy beat Hungary 4-2 in the final.

"Are there any good examples of unusual squad numbering?"

To blatantly misquote Clint Eastwood, quirky numbers are like foibles: almost every team's got one. And they have been especially commonplace since the advent of squad numbers in 1993. Until then, you had to look to the World Cup: in 1978 and 1982, Argentina numbered their squad alphabetically, so the No1 and No2 shirt went to the outfield players Norberto Alonso and Ossie Ardiles, respectively. Holland had started that trend in 1974, from Ruud Geels (No1) to Harry Vos (No22), via the goalkeeper Jan Jongbloed (No8) – with one inevitable exception. Johan Cruyff, who should have worn No1, was allowed to wear his trademark No14 (what's more, Cruyff was even allowed wear a different strip to the rest of the team; his jersey had two stripes down the arm rather than one because he had a separate sponsorship deal).

If such an avant-garde approach to numbering was typical of Holland's Total Footballing ethos, the same can't exactly be said of the first English side to adopt the same procedure: Charlton Athletic, who had their Scottish defender Stuart Balmer wearing No1 in the mid-nineties.

However, especially for your delectation, here's our comprehensive-ish list:

0 Even Bruce Forsyth would not have suggested going lower than No1, but yes, it has happened. Between 1999 and 2002 Aberdeen's Moroccan striker, Hicham Zerouali obtained special dispensation from the SPL to wear it because Zero was his nickname.

1 Clearly the obvious number for any club's first-choice goalkeeper, though, as mentioned earlier, not always.

2 Traditionally the number worn by a right-back. Famous wearers of this number have been Phil Neal and Gary Neville, along with Mike Duxbury.

3 Our pick for the most prominent No3 is predictably, as well as justifiably, Paolo Maldini. The AC Milan legend has worn it throughout his career and rumour has it that the imprint is actually visible on his back.

4 Has to be one of the dullest numbers on the pitch. A straw poll revealed Ronald Koeman as the archetypal No4 – filling the sweeper role in the dream Holland side of the late eighties and early nineties.

5 Only Franz Beckenbauer can claim this shirt, despite also wearing No6 on occasion. The Liverpool sides of the seventies and eighties broke with tradition and gave this number to midfielders, including Ray Kennedy and Ronnie Whelan.

6 As football icons go, Bobby Moore has to be right up there with the best. Indeed his No6 shirt has now been retired by West Ham, who felt "there was only one true gesture that would do him justice".

7　For Manchester United fans, No7 is the number of George Best, Eric Cantona and David Beckham. Try to take that number from Cristiano Ronaldo and he would be off faster than you could wink. At Liverpool, it was the number of Kevin Keegan, Kenny Dalglish and Peter Beardsley.

8　Ian Wright, Wright, Wright wore No8 with total pride throughout his Arsenal career on his way to a scoring record and the fans' hearts, before undoing all his good work with Friday Night's All Wright, Friends Like These, What Kids Really Think, Wright Across America, Gladiators and International Match of the Day to name but a few misguided vehicles.

9　From Jackie Milburn to Alan Shearer, No9 is the number of Newcastle's front man. It is also the number of Ronaldo. When he moved to Inter, he took the number from Ivan Zamorano, prompting the Chilean to spit his dummy and famously wear 1+8 as a protest.

10　Fighting with No7 for top billing in the mythology of football, No10 possibly shades it: Pele, Maradona, Rivera, Platini, Puskás, Zidane – need we say more?

11　Surely this is the number of the tricky winger. The most recent example of the No11 is Ryan Giggs, whose shirt number is almost as iconic as his chest wig.

And outside the first XI . . .

12　In the days of one substitute, this was the number worn by "super-sub" David Fairclough. He made this number his own, which has to be a dubious claim to fame. Marco van

Basten wore 12 when he scored *that* goal in the 1988 European Championships against Russia, though Van Basten diluted his claim for iconic status by wearing No9 in the 1990 World Cup. In more recent times it has become the squad number reserved for the 12th man – the fans – by many clubs, except . . .

13 Reading gave No13 to their fans, just to be different. It wasn't an unlucky number for Gerd Müller, who wore it in 1974 as his goals carried West Germany to the World Cup title.

14 The aforementioned Dutch genius Johan Cruyff always wore No14, even when the rest of the squad were numbered alphabetically. When you're that good, no one is going to argue over your squad number. It was also the number worn by Thierry Henry during his goal machine years at Arsenal.

16 Manchester United fans will permanently associate this with the mild-mannered and softly spoken Roy Keane.

19 Paul Gascoigne at Italia 90. Many fans associate this number with the man who became an international star at the World Cup. Since then, it has been worn by: Les Ferdinand (1998), Joe Cole (2002) and Aaron Lennon (2006), so maybe it still belongs to Gazza.

20 Paolo Rossi came back from a suspension for his involvement in a betting scandal to score six goals as Italy won the World Cup in Spain in 1982.

23 Already an iconic No7 for Man Utd and England, David Beckham has been a marketing icon for Real Madrid and Los Angeles Galaxy wearing No23.

40 In the first season of Premiership squad numbers (1993-94) Lee Chapman became the first player to wear

No40 when he signed for West Ham.

69 The Bayern Munich full-back Bixente Lizarazu slithered up and down the left flank with No69 on his back. It's not as cringeworthy as it seems, however: Lizarazu, believe it or not, was born in 1969, is 169cm tall and weighs 69 kg. Mrs Lizarazu was unavailable for comment with regard to any further coincidence.

88 Gigi Buffon, the most expensive keeper in history, chose this number one season, sparking controversy. The number is associated with fascism in Italy and Buffon had previously been seen sporting a T-shirt with the fascist slogan "death to those who surrender". He denied any links to fascism and the number was swiftly changed.

99 The highest number allowed by Fifa under current regulations. Vitor Baia was the first man to wear this when Porto won the European Cup final of 2004.

100 Guadalajara's Adolfo Bautista wears this number only for domestic matches in Mexico; Fifa rules mean he can't sport three figures in Copa Libertadores matches.

111 In 2006, the Flamengo striker Luizão sported this number several times to commemorate the club's 111th year of existence.

400 Goias goalkeeper Harley apparently celebrated his 400th appearance for the club by raising the bar ...

618 ... but the highest recorded number appears to be that of São Paulo's goalscoring goalkeeper Rogério Ceni, who marked his club-record-breaking 618th appearance with a rather special jersey with the corresponding number on it.

"I was idly leafing through a reference book the other day and came across a reference to Third Lanark doing something (getting relegated, I think) in 1965. This surprised me as I had always taken that name to be rather like the Wanderers in England – a name in the early records, but long out of existence. What happened to them?"

What happened to them indeed. As you suspected, Third Lanark were relegated at the end of the 1964-65 Scottish First Division campaign, losing a spectacular 30 of their 34 matches and ending up with seven points. Sadly, within two years, the club was declared bankrupt, thrown out of the league, and dissolved in the courts. Just how the club ended up like that was never properly ascertained – fans still claim boardroom corruption to this day – but the net result was plain enough, and the death knell sounded after a 2-2 draw away to Stranraer in 1967. Thirty-four years on, they're still the last Scottish club to go under.

It was a sorry end to the scarlet-shirted Glasgow club, which had enjoyed no little success in the early years of Scottish football. The Third Lanarkshire Volunteers – also known as Third Lanark, Thirds, the Warriors, and the Hi-Hi – were founder members of the Scottish League, and won the championship in 1904 and the Scottish Cup in 1889 and 1905 (beating Celtic and Rangers, respectively). Their odd nickname of the Hi-Hi can, we think, be attributed to the fact that their ground, Cathkin Park, enjoyed spectacular views of Glasgow, situated as it was on a rocky knoll in the south side of the city. The site of the ground is now a municipal park, and some of the terracing still exists. Frankly, it's a bit eerie.

"Which team in the current Premier League has been in the top flight the longest?"

Liverpool were promoted in 1963, and haven't slummed it in the meantime, while neighbours Everton have held their top-flight status ever since 1954, despite their best efforts during the 90s. Then there's Arsenal. They were promoted from the old Second Division in 1919 and have never been away since. But, predictably, given that they hold the record for current top-flight longevity, the nature of their promotion that year is controversial, to say the least.

In 1919, the First Division was extended from 20 to 22 clubs. During previous expansions, the relegated clubs from the previous season were re-elected, while the top Second Division sides were promoted as usual. So Derby and Preston, the two top Second Division sides in 1915 – there had been a break for the war – did indeed move on up. And Chelsea, who had finished 19th that season, were, as expected, re-elected.

But the reason for Chelsea's escape were somewhat arbitrary. In 1915, Manchester United had – to avoid relegation – fixed their last game (against Liverpool of all people). They won 2-0 and sent Chelsea into the relegation places instead, but Liverpool's chairman John McKenna must have felt some guilt, because at the League's AGM in 1919 he gave a speech insisting on the continued presence in the top tier of the Stamford Bridge club.

Under what was perceived to be pressure from the canny Arsenal chairman, Sir Henry Norris, he also suggested that the lowly Gunners, who had finished fifth in the Second, should be rewarded for their long service to the League; they should replace the team which came 20th in 1915, he argued. And so it came to pass. The relegated club? Why, Tottenham Hotspur, of course.

"Has an English club ever come close to fielding an all-Scottish eleven?"

Yes they have. Liverpool fielded an all-Scottish eleven in their first ever competitive match in 1892 (after forming when Everton quit Anfield for Goodison Park earlier that year). According to the official Liverpool FC website, "It was virtually unheard of at the time for a city to have more than one professional football team, and people naturally wondered where on earth Liverpool's players would come from. John McKenna, the club's first manager, provided the answer: Scotland. All 11 players of the Liverpool team against Higher Walton on September 3 1892 were Scottish."

More recently, Liverpool famously fielded a non-English XI for the 1986 FA Cup final against Everton: Bruce Grobbelaar, Mark Lawrenson, Jim Beglin, Steve Nicol, Ronnie Whelan, Alan Hansen, Kenny Dalglish, Craig Johnston, Ian Rush, Jan Mølby and Kevin MacDonald came from behind to win 3-1.

And if you wanted any further evidence that foreign can be fantastic, look at Chelsea. On December 26 1999, they played Southampton with 11 overseas players – the first time an English league side had fielded a starting line-up without a single British player. With Graeme Le Saux injured, Chris Sutton suffering from flu, and Dennis Wise's wife due to give birth, boss Gianluca Vialli started with Ed de Goey, Albert Ferrer, Celestine Babayaro, Emerson Thome, Frank Leboeuf, Dan Petrescu, Gus Poyet, Didier Deschamps, Roberto Di Matteo, Tore Andre Flo and Gabriele Ambrosetti. And the players did Vialli proud, with two first-half goals from Flo helping Chelsea to a 2-1 victory.

"Has a player ever been sent off in their own testimonial?"

Not that we know of, but that's not to say there haven't been a few close shaves.

Undoubtedly the most violent and probably most entertaining testimonial ever was that for Julian Dicks – which was brilliantly marred by a 17-man punch-up shortly before half-time, though Dicks wasn't even on the pitch at the time. West Ham fans, who had earlier complained about "extortionate" ticket prices for the game with Athletic Bilbao, were treated to a Paolo di Canio-inspired ruck of mass proportions which broke out after Nigel Winterburn's wild challenge sent Joseba Etxeberria sprawling into the touchline hoardings. The Italian was eventually persuaded to stop fighting and "asked" to leave the pitch, and though nobody cared about the result, history will record that the visitors went on to win 2-1.

While no players were technically red-carded at West Ham, plenty of players have been sent off in testimonials. Robbie Williams, of all people, who lined up for Port Vale against Aston Villa, was dismissed for dissent in Dean Glover's testimonial.

"Has a goalkeeper ever been sent off during a penalty shootout?"

The Botswana goalkeeper and captain Modiri Marumo was sent off during a Castle Cup shootout against Malawi in May 2003. Having been booked for time-wasting before Malawi scored their third spot-kick, Marumo – according to an AFP report – "reacted to a pat on the shoulder from opposite number Philip Nyasulu by punching him in the face and got a red card". Malawi went on to win 4-1 and reach the semi-finals. "I over reacted in an exchange of words between myself and my counterpart," admitted Marumo. "This unbecoming behaviour has not only embarrassed me, but also the organisation that I work for, the Botswana Defence Force (BDF). I hope my apology would be recognised and I pledge my commitment in serving the nation."

"Can anyone remember what David Coleman said when introducing the Battle of Santiago? It has to be the best intro ever."

The Battle of Santiago we assume you're referring to, is the World Cup match between hosts Chile and Italy in June 1962 – and not the clash between American and Spanish naval forces of 1898 which saw nearly 2,000 Spaniards die on the beaches. Both, however, were particularly bloody affairs. When the match was shown on BBC television, David Coleman introduced the Group B game thus: "Good evening. The game you are about to see is the most stupid, appalling, disgusting and disgraceful exhibition of football, possibly in the history of the game."

And he wasn't far off. Tensions were running high beforehand as two Italian journalists, Antonio Ghiredelli and Corrado Pizzinelli, had spent weeks labelling Santiago a poverty-stricken dump full of loose women (they left the country before the tournament started), and the game immediately kicked off after the official kick-off. The first foul came within 12 seconds. Then, eight minutes later, Italy's Giorgio Ferrini was sent off, refused to leave the pitch, and was subsequently dragged off, kicking and screaming, by a group of policemen. It took another eight minutes for the game to restart. But worse was to follow when Chilean Leonel Sánchez, the son of a professional boxer, responded to a series of kicks from Mario David by flattening him. As Cris Freddi relates in his *Complete Book of the World Cup*, "after referee Ken Aston did nothing, David took things into his own hands, getting himself sent off for kicking Sanchez in the neck". (Still, at least the two players became "great friends" when they later played at Milan.)

More followed. Italian Humberto Maschio was punched on the nose (reports state it was either Sanchez or Eladio Rojas) – a moment that the BBC commentator, in classic old-school style, claimed: "I say, that was one of the neatest left hooks I've ever seen!" Jorge Toro should also have gone for raising his fists in the final minute. At the end of the game, which Chile won 2-0, inventor of the red and yellow card system Aston admitted: "I wasn't reffing a football match, I was acting as an umpire in military manoeuvres." He wasn't wrong.

"What is the earliest time a professional match has ever kicked off?"

During the 2003-04 season, Barcelona were scheduled to play a midweek game against Sevilla prior to an international weekend. Since Fifa's rules stipulated that players summoned for international duty must be released by their clubs four days before the match, Barça hoped to stage the game on the September 3, rather than the next day when their internationals would have been missing. However, sensing a chance to take on a below-strength opponent, Sevilla refused, pointing out that a club could not play two matches within 48 hours (after the Sunday fixture programme), unless both teams were agreed.

Quick-thinking suits at Camp Nou then hit upon a novel idea: play the game as early on Wednesday morning as possible and hope their international stars would still be allowed to play. Thus, the game kicked off at 12.05am. Alas, the only national association to accept

Barça's ploy was Portugal's, which allowed winger Ricardo Quaresma to take part.

Eighty thousand fans turned up . . . though it probably helped that the club laid on free gaspacho and 100,000 complimentary Kit Kats. Also, stand-up comics entertained the crowd before live telephone link-ups with Ronald Koeman and Hristo Stoichkov worked them into a frenzy. The players ran out to the Village People's YMCA, but it clearly worked, as the supporters only hushed once during the match, when José Antonio Reyes' penalty gave the visitors the lead. Ronaldinho's first goal for the club – spectacular, naturally – salvaged a 1-1 draw, the roar greeting his strike reportedly registering on the city's earthquake monitors.

"With George Weah once running for president of Liberia, have any other former national team skippers gone on to captain their nation?"

Not exactly, but we can come pretty close in former semi-professional footballer Recep Tayyip Erdogan – now the prime minister of Turkey. Erdogan played for 16 years before giving up the game in 1980 to work in the private sector, eventually becoming leader of the Justice and Development party and being elected as PM in 2003. Brazilian legends are no strangers to public office, either. Famously, Pele served as the country's minister of sport between 1995 and 1998, while Zico also briefly occupied this role after his retirement in 1990. Forty-fags-a-day striker Socrates also dipped his toe into the politics pool as a member of the Workers' party.

Dinamo Kyiv and Soviet Union striker Oleh Blokhin also enjoyed the best of both worlds. Upon ending his playing days in 1997, the former European Player of the Year became a communist member of the Ukrainian parliament; in 2003, he was appointed as the country's national coach. But political opponents claimed such a dual mandate was illegal, so Blokhin later resigned. The president of the football federation, however, was desperate to reinstate him, what with Ukraine being on the verge of their first ever World Cup qualification, and took the matter to court. A judge subsequently ruled that Blokhin could indeed manage the country and be a parliamentarian at the same time, so less than a month later he took the reins anew. And, of course, to complete the happy ending, Ukraine became the first European side (after Germany, naturally) to qualify for the 2006 World Cup.

The former Belgian international Marc Wilmots was another to mix football and politics simultaneously, albeit with less success. The Liberal senator was sacked as St Truiden manager after barely 10 months in the job. Closer to home, former first minister of Scotland, Henry McLeish, once played for East Fife, while one-time Arsenal player, Albert Gudmundsson, returned to his native Iceland and ran for president in 1980, but lost.

Ex-Croatia coach Miroslav Blazevic (recently in charge of NK Zagreb) was no more successful. "I hope to overthrow [president] Stjepan Mesic, whom I have never liked very much," he brazenly declared before running as a Veteran's party (SHB) candidate in the 2005 Croatian elections. Blazevic collected the sum total of 17,847 votes (0.80%) in the first round and was duly eliminated from the contest.

"Other than Kaiser Chiefs, St Etienne and (the more obscure) Van Basten, are there any other bands named after football clubs, players or managers?"

More than you can shake a drumstick at. First up are the French "blues, pop and high-energy groove" band Aston Villa, who hail from the suburbs of Paris and have been on the scene since 1994. Not to be outdone, Premier League rivals Arsenal have lent their name to a Belgian dance-salsa band, while Manchester United were Mick Hucknall's inspiration for Simply Red.

Casting the net slightly wider, there is the Welsh "lounge-core" group Dynamo Dresden, the Georgia-based garage-soul band Red Star Belgrade, plus DJ collective Bocca Juniors [sic]. Sham 69 were named after a piece of graffiti on a wall celebrating Walton & Hersham's successful 1969 season. Part of the wall having disappeared, the band adopted what was left. There's also dance outfit Enzo Scifo, Seattle band Cantona and the Welsh language musings of Ian Rush. Posters for the Leeds festival in 2001 had a "Jimmy Floyd Hasselbaink" on the bottom of the bill, though whether this was an in-joke by promoters we're not sure.

Managers don't seem to engender the same inspiration. But the Crewe Alexandra legend Dario Gradi can rightly claim to be the muse for DJ trio Dario G, which includes Crewe native Paul Spencer.

Their Carnaval de Paris track went on to become the theme for World Cup 98 and can still be heard around European grounds to this very day.

"With regard to Liverpool's success in the 2005 Champions League, has a team ever won the European Cup while performing so badly in their domestic league in the same season?"

There are several factors to take into consideration, none of which include the fact Liverpool won the Champions League with Harry Kewell, Djimi Traore, Igor Biscan, etc. Purely on a points basis, the distance they finished behind domestic champions Chelsea [38] does appear to mark them out as the worst European Cup winners in history.

However, that's perhaps a tad unfair given the external details [quality of champions, fixtures in a season, etc], so instead we'll rely purely upon league position, for which reason Aston Villa's 1981-82 domestic season current resides in the record books. Just five days after Tony Barton's team beat Swansea to finish a dismal Division One campaign in 12th spot [42 games: 15 wins, 12 draws, 15 defeats, +2 goal difference], they overcame Bayern Munich 1-0 to win the European Cup. Bayern, it transpires, claim the second-worst finish and the only one with a record under 50%, after their miserable

Bundesliga campaign of 1974-75. They finished 10th [34 games: 14 wins, six draws, 14 defeats, -6 goal difference], but still managed to beat Leeds 2-0 and win their second of three consecutive European Cup trophies.

"What is the strangest item to be lobbed from terrace to pitch?"

When it comes to the weirdest object ever thrown from the stands, there is only one winner: the scooter that Internazionale supporters stole from an Atalanta fan outside the San Siro in May 2001, then smuggled into the stadium (past rigorous security checks, clearly), set on fire and tossed from the second tier on to a thankfully empty section of the lower stand. OK, so the scooter didn't actually make it on to the pitch, but that was the intention.

"Many years ago, I remember being told that James Kennaway, a Celtic goalkeeper, appeared in internationals for Scotland, the United States and Canada. Is this true, and if so, how did he achieve this?"

It's partially true. As Blair James of the Scottish Football Museum explains, "James (Joe) Kennaway was a

Canadian who played for Canada against US in Brooklyn in 1926. He starred against a touring Celtic team in 1931 and was signed by them to replace the late John Thompson, tragically killed during an Old Firm match [after fracturing his skull]. Kennaway played once for Scotland against Austria in 1933 and played in the Scottish League on four occasions. But then objections were made about a Canadian playing for Scotland. There's no evidence of him representing the USA though."

Not that Kennaway's case was unusual. Country swapping was a common occurrence until the 1960s, when Fifa changed its laws to bring an end to the practice of switching allegiances (for the sake of space constraints, we'll ignore the numerous players who played for a second country – and, in the case of some former USSR and CIS internationals, a third country – after their first one(s) disintegrated).

Some of the most famous examples include the *oriundi* – South Americans who grew up in and played for their native countries before being bought by Italian clubs and capped by Italy because of their dual nationality. As the writer Brian Glanville explains, "Italy's [1934 World Cup] winning team had three essential Argentinians – Luisito Monti, the ruthless attacking centre-half who had played for Argentina in the 1930 World Cup final, Enrique Guaita, the right winger, and Raimondo Orsi on the left. 'If they can die for Italy,' Vittorio Pozzo, the coach, proclaimed somewhat disingenuously, 'they can play for Italy!' – meaning that they were subject to military call-up. But when war was declared against Abyssinia in 1935, Guaita and other *oriundi* were caught sneaking over the border to Switzerland. Play, yes. Die, no!"

It wasn't just Italy who took full advantage of the laws. In the 1940s, Alfredo di Stéfano represented not only his native Argentina, but also Colombia and Spain. After making his name in Argentina, a players' strike prompted a move to Colombia's renegade Di Mayor league, which was out of Fifa's jurisdiction, meaning no transfer fees and massive salaries. Eventually the Colombian national team called him up for international duty, although his four caps were deemed unofficial because of the Colombian FA's falling-out with Fifa. From Millonarios, Di Stéfano switched to Real Madrid, where he collected five European Cups, the Intercontinental Cup and, finally, a trip to the 1962 World Cup with Spain.

Another name carved in Madrid folklore, Ferenc Puskás, also played for both Spain and his homeland, Hungary. At the time of the Hungarian uprising against their Soviet suppressors in 1956, Puskás and his Honved team-mates were playing a European Cup tie in Bilbao; he chose to defect – along with Sandor Kocsis and Zoltán Czibor – and eventually arrived at the Bernabéu in 1958. László Kubala, a Hungarian international who was voted Barcelona's greatest ever player, also pulled on the national shirts of both Czechoslovakia and Spain.

Four England internationals went on to represent other countries – and there are also nine unofficial instances. The England Football Online website describes how John (Jack) Reynolds (England and Ireland), John Hawley Edwards (England and Wales), Robert (Bobby) Ernest Evans (England and Wales), and Kenneth (Ken) Armstrong (England and New Zealand) all picked up caps for more than one nation. Cris Freddi's *The England Football Fact Book* adds that there were three other close calls, including the case of Alex Donaldson. "On his way [in January 1914] to an England international trial game at Sunderland, Alex Donaldson of Bolton Wanderers revealed that he was actually born in Scotland," writes Freddi. "[Charles W.] Wallace of Aston Villa had to take his place in the trial and Donaldson ended up in the Scottish side which faced England on April 4 of the same year [winning 3-1]!"

"I was reading an old history book that claimed Crystal Palace sent more men to the second world war than any other English team. Is this correct?"

According to Jack Rollin's book, *Soccer at War 1939-45*, a total of 98 men were dispatched from Palace to serve in the conflict, seven more than Wolves in second place. At the beginning of the war, Palace were playing in Division

Three South, although in the following years, they took part in the South Regional League, the London League and the Football League South. Next up on the list were Liverpool with 76 men sent to serve, then Chester with 69, Luton (68), Huddersfield (65), Leicester (63), Charlton (62), Oldham (60) and Grimsby (58).

"Who is the cheapest player to have been sold in modern football (not counting free transfers)?"

After being passed up by Millwall, Tony Cascarino was plucked from the obscurity of Crockenhill FC and placed into the obscurity of Gillingham FC in 1982 – for a new strip and some training equipment. "It's one of those stories, it's just been exaggerated over time, going from 10 tracksuits to a few cones, and all the rest," recalled Cascarino. "It's like the two loaves and five fishes in the Bible. That's what I call it: the two loaves and five fishes." The irony is that six years and 76 goals later, the big striker was snapped up by none other than Millwall – for £200,000.

But the winner of this dubious title appears to be Romanian defender Marius Cioara, who was sold in 2006 by Second Division outfit UT Arad to Fourth Division side Regal Hornia for the princely sum of . . . 15 kilos of pork sausages! "We gave up the team's sausage allowance for a week to secure him, but we are confident it will be worth it," revealed a Regal spokesman. However, the deal went sour within 24 hours when Cioara decided he had endured enough bangers-related ribbing to last a lifetime and promptly retired. "The sausage taunts all got too much, they were joking I would have got more from the Germans and making sausage jokes," he moaned. "It was a huge insult. I have decided to go to Spain where I have got a job on a farm." Hopefully away from the pigs. Regal were less than chuffed as they wheeled out their spokesman for a final lament: "We are upset because we lost twice. Firstly because we lost a good player, and secondly because we lost our team's food for a whole week."

"Should the 1966 World Cup semi-final between England and Portugal have been played at Villa Park as opposed to Wembley?"

According to the book *England: The Quest for the World Cup*, written by Clive Leatherdale, "Controversy attended the choice of venue for the semi-final. The pre-tournament blurb stated that this particular semi-final, irrespective of who would contest it, would be staged at Goodison Park. Some punters had bought tickets in advance in the expectation that if England were still in the running they would be heading for Merseyside. Fifa's organising committee now insisted that it had all along reserved the right to reallocate the semi-final venues. Portugal had been based in the north-west zone and had beaten Brazil and North Korea at Everton. England, on the other hand, had yet to move from Wembley. Understandably, neither team was enthusiastic about switching. Wembley was eventually selected on the grounds that the national stadium could accommodate more spectators than Goodison." England won 2-1 in front of 95,000 fans, before going on to claim the World Cup trophy four days later.

"What is the arcane manner in which World Cup referees are chosen? Why do each of the FAs that make it to the finals have to send a refereeing team?"

Well, the second part of the question is rather straightforward: they don't. Which, in 2006 at least, was good news for Benin's Coffi Codjia, Singapore's Shamsul Maidin, Belgium's Franck De Bleeckere, Russia's Valentin Ivanov and Uruguay's Jorge Larrionda, among others. The first part, however, is a far muddier business.

In January 2005, the Fifa Referees' Committee, responsible for all international appointments, selected a shortlist of 46 officials who were to be candidates for refereeing at the 2006 World Cup. Those officials were chosen from Fifa's International Referees List, an annually updated group of elite men in black. The criteria used in the selection process is not clear, but those referees chosen took part in workshops in February and June of that year, and officiated in Fifa tournaments, giving the governing body the chance to assess and monitor them on a regular basis. Still with us? The candidates were under observation throughout 2005, with Fifa analysing every domestic appearance and international run-out.

The final stage involved the shortlisted candidates meeting in Frankfurt in March 2006 for four days of "rigorous testing", including exhaustive medical checks, psychological testing, a series of physical tests and a final interview before members of the Referees' Committee. The Committee then met to decide the final 23.

Fifa takes up the story: "When making their decision, the committee members evaluated the performances of the candidates during Fifa competitions, continental championships and in national leagues over the past 18 months. The referees' performances at the two Fifa workshops in Frankfurt were likewise taken into account, as the match officials were subject to close scrutiny from February 12-16 2005 and again from March 21-25 2006." Or, in Graham Poll's case, not quite close enough.

"Apart from Josip Simunic in the 2006 Australia-Croatia match, has any other player in a World Cup been awarded three yellow cards in a single match before being shown the red card?"

Not quite, although the Iranian referee Jafar Namdar came mighty close at the 1974 finals. Late on, during an ill-tempered game between Australia and Chile, Namdar booked Ray Richards for time-wasting over a free-kick. Absent-mindedly forgetting he had already booked Richards in the first half, Namdar happily trotted off to leave Richards thinking it was his lucky day. Ultimately, his efforts to remain inconspicuous failed: four minutes later, an irate Fifa official arrived on the touchline, informing the linesman of Namdar's mistake. Cue some mad flagging, Australian protestation and eventual dismissal for Richards.

"Following Niall Quinn's stint as the chairmanager of Sunderland, I wondered just how many other chairmen have held similar roles?"

Ron Noades is one such example, during a spell with Brentford between 1998 and 2000. "I wanted to manage. I wanted to decide myself who I wanted to buy, and the big advantage of doing both roles is that you speed up the process so much," he explained. "I could buy a player within 24 hours when other clubs were talking about sending out their chief scout to see them, after that the manager, and then after that trying to persuade the chairman to buy him. While they were still poncing about, I'd bought him." Noades' tenure ended bitterly, though, with the vast majority of Bees supporters still holding him in particularly low regard.

Notoriously, Barry Fry spent nine years from 1996 to 2005 as chairmanager of Peterborough United, presiding over one promotion and two relegations. He is still the director of football at London Road, but has retired from dancing dementedly down the touchline, leaving all that to Darren Ferguson.

"Who was the first English player to play professionally abroad?"

The man in question is Herbert Kilpin, who played for Notts Olympic and Saint Andrews before joining FC Torinese in 1891, then Mediolanum Milano from 1898 to 1900 and Milan from 1900-07. But Kilpin's defining moment came in a Tuscan wine shop in 1899 when, together with five colleagues from a Nottingham lace company, he founded the Milan Cricket and Football Club – now known as AC Milan. "We will wear red and black," said Kilpin. "Red to recall the devil, black to invoke fear."

"Is Philippine-born Paulino Alcántara really Barcelona's all-time top scorer, as claimed on the website of the Philippine Football Federation?"

He certainly is, with a phenomenal record of 356 goals in 357 games for the Catalans between 1912 and 1927. Prolific Paulino, who was born in Iloilo City to Spanish parents in 1896 and was one of the first Asian-born footballers to play for a European club, also remains Barcelona's youngest ever goalscorer after slotting home a hat-trick on his debut against Catalá SC at the fair age of 15. "His ability to hit the most powerful of shots crossed frontiers on April 30 1922 when, in a game between Spain and France, he hit a shot so hard that it ripped right through the net," explains the club's website. "For many years after, children from Barcelona would recall that moment and would wish to do the same as the man from the Philippines."

It should be noted that Alcántara's achievements may have been helped by the fact Barcelona played in an exclusively Catalan league at that time, rather than the modern-day La Liga, but they have never been seriously threatened. He also played for both the Philippines and Spain, but only a handful of times for each since he preferred to prioritise his medical studies ahead of his career. His boots remain on show in the club's museum.

"I seem to remember a story in the Spanish press when Mohamed Sissoko was at Valencia which said that he told his manager on international week that he had been called up, when this was totally untrue. Apparently he even had the cheek to say he scored a goal in the match. Are there any other funny stories of players skiving when they should be at matches?"

Oh, it's true. Well, sort of. After a World Cup qualifier against Senegal in September 2005, the Mali international told Valencia he'd be staying at home to play in a friendly against Kenya. Upon his return, he revealed that he'd played 48 minutes in a 1-0 win (he wasn't cheeky enough to claim the goal for himself, as that would be a bit *too* implausible), a declaration that turned out to be a big fib – he'd actually been in Paris visiting his father, who was ill in hospital. When Claudio Ranieri, then manager of Valencia, discovered the deceit he saw the funny side and told Sissoko that the club would have happily given him the time off anyway.

More recently, France international Youri Djorkaeff found himself with some explaining to do when he told club officials at New York Red Bulls that he had to return to France to attend to a serious family matter. The domestic crisis in question? Enthusiastically celebrating France's World Cup quarter-final win over

Brazil in Frankfurt, Germany, where he was caught red-handed by TV cameras.

The former Stoke striker Sammy Bangoura ended an unexplained 37-day absence and returned to the club having missed pre-season training in 2006. Rumoured to have been at home in his native Guinea, Bangoura's absence infuriated the Potters so much that they stopped paying his wages while he was away. The 24-year-old striker – twice previously late returning to the club from his homeland ("He has totally no respect for anyone. If I was a player, not a manager, I would kick him in his balls," raged boss Johan Boskamp in 2005) – eventually reported for duty the day before Stoke's first game of the season at Southend, claiming that an immigration wrangle involving his baby daughter had caused the delay.

"I remember reading, maybe as much as a decade ago, that the Chinese authorities had assembled a squad of their 22 finest young footballers and sent them to Brazil, to live there permanently and so grow up immersed in Brazilian football culture. What happened to those guys?"

You remember rightly. The Chinese government sent the Jianlibao youth team to Brazil in 1993 for a five-year training programme under the guidance of a man called Zhu Guanghu, who later coached the national side. It was no vanity project either, and one of the youngsters, Li Tie, played for Everton and Sheffield United, before moving to Chinese sister club Chengdu Blades. Several others, including Li Jinyu and Li Weifeng (who also had trials at Everton), have played for the national side. "It was the most important time of my football career when I was in Brazil," said Li Weifeng of his two years' training. "What I learned there was more than what I got from my five-year spell at the domestic league in China."

The Chinese Football Association couldn't have been too disappointed with the results, as they have repeated the venture in Germany. Twenty-seven promising youngsters took part in a two-year training camp with the German coach Eckhard Krautzun in Bad Kissingen. Krautzun, who previously steered Canada and Tunisia to World Cup berths, worked on moulding the "2008-Star Team" into a group to form the core of China's football squad for the 2008 Olympics. "There should be and must be an aim for Chinese football to win a medal at the 2008 Olympics on home soil," said Krautzun. They didn't

"While I was watching Brazilian league football, it appeared that once the referee had set the wall for a free-kick, he took out an aerosol and sprayed a line on the pitch. Did I dream this?"

It transpires that Brazilian football fan and chemist Heine Allemagne, along with Vilarinho Dias, are to thank for inventing a high-tech spray in 2000. The referees carry a small aerosol can – or one is brought out to them – so that whenever a defensive wall needs to be formed near the penalty area, they can spray the foam and mark out the 10 yards that players must retreat. As if by magic, the dye evaporates from the grass within 60 seconds. United States patent No7074264 (Foaming aqueous composition, use thereof and process for

temporary demarcation of regulation distances in sports) details that "the present invention is biodegradable, non-toxic, non-inflammable, residue-free, non-skin damaged and does not damage grasses or others floors. The propellant gas does not affect ozone layer since it does not contain chlorofluorocarbon."

It was first used in the São Paulo State Championship in 2001, with the Brazilian Football Confederation and state federations then extending its usage around the country. But despite proving a highly effective tool in upholding the rules of the game, Fifa remains unconvinced as to its necessity and is yet to take the idea worldwide.

"Have any teams ever failed to switch sides for the second half of a football match?"

Surprisingly they have, with Messina's Serie A visit to Reggina in March 2005 a notable example. As the teams emerged for the second half, fans behind the goal Messina were set to defend launched a barrage of missiles at the visiting keeper Marco Storari, forcing the referee Massimo De Santis to initially delay the restart by 10 minutes and eventually order the two teams to return to the ends they had used in the first period. More recently, Arsenal and Ajax failed to switch ends during Dennis Bergkamp's testimonial at Emirates Stadium;

this was most likely a simple case of forgetfulness, as both teams' entire line-ups were replaced with "legends"at half-time.

"Following Xabi Alonso's wonder strikes against Luton Town and Newcastle, I was wondering whether any other player has scored from his own half twice?"

Step forward fellow Spaniard Roger García, who can point to an even more incredible long-distance scoring record; during a 12-month period in 2002 and 2003, García managed to score three times from inside his own half. In October 2002, García – then playing for Espanyol – scored the first of his remarkable hat-trick against Recreativo Huelva. Six months later, García repeated the trick during Espanyol's win at Rayo Vallecano, before rounding off his amazing treble by scoring from the centre circle for Villarreal during a Uefa Cup game against Galatasaray early in the 2003-04 season.

"You need to spot the keeper off his line before trying it, judge your direction and power perfectly and hope the wind is with you," explained García. "Then you must pray that it goes in because you feel stupid and people criticise you otherwise. It's a beautiful goal to score and, although it only counts the same as one which trickles in from one metre, this is the kind of thing I've dreamed of doing since I was a young boy. You grow up knowing that not many people can do it; you try it and succeed a couple of times and then it starts to feel really special."

"Please help me settle a long-running argument with a German know-it-all. Is Real Madrid's Bernabéu stadium pronounced 'berna-bow', 'berna-bay-oo' or something entirely different?"

"Essentially, it's the second one," said Sid Lowe, the Guardian's Spanish football expert. "The thing about Spanish is that every vowel gets pronounced (except in certain combinations where they can sound like they are are running together – "ua" can sound like "wa", especially after a G, for example). So, the E and the U at the end there are both heard. And the vowel sounds are pretty much as they are in English, just shorter (A = ah, E = eh (not ee), I = ee, O = oh, U = oo). The other thing is that the e has an accent on it which doesn't change the sound but makes it the letter that is stressed. So it's BernabEu. To put that in a pronounciation – Bernabayoo is basically right, but as the vowel sounds are a bit shorter, I'd prefer: Berna-bEh-oo (without that oooh being elongated)." So, er, now you know.

"What was the name of the manager captured on the mid-90s documentary Orient: Club for a Fiver? He was the one who was giving a team talk and, in a Ron Manager-style outburst, warned two of his players: 'We'll have a right old tear-up, and you can bring your mates and you can bring your dinner'."

The quote isn't strictly correct – you missed out 471 expletives, for a start – but the lyrical legend in question is John Sitton, the Leyton Orient joint-manager between August 1994 and April 1995, whose team talks were so foul that he made Barry Fry seem like Immanuel Kant. His portfolio includes these gems (which can be viewed in their expletive-ridden entirety on YouTube):

"You've all gotta go. You've all gotta go. Any of yer on 35 grand and all that, you've all gotta go. He [the chairman] wants to bring players in on 250 quid a week. He might be right! I think he is right! You're a disgrace!

"When I tell ya to do summink, do it. And if ya come back at me, we'll have a right sort-out in here, all right? And you can pair up if ya like, and you can pick someone else to hold yer hand and you can bring yer fakkin dinner, cos by the time I'm finished with yer you'll need it."

Sitton's meal ticket was taken away when he was sacked because of a miserable P47 W7 D9 L31 record, but he was later immortalised in the documentary Orient: Club for a Fiver, which told the story of the dire

1994-95 season in which the club was relegated and bought for the price of a Tube ticket by Barry Hearn. Indeed, he became such a cult figure that an online petition was launched to get him back into football. However, Sitton is now self-employed as a black cab driver and also works part-time for the Press Association compiling statistics for the Opta Index. He has had just three jobs in football since leaving Leyton Orient and admitted he was stunned at how quickly football turned its back on him after the documentary. "I made in excess of 60 applications for different jobs, all unsuccessful, and by the end I was very bitter, twisted and disillusioned," he told us. "But I got caught out using the kind of language that is now accepted everywhere and which has earned Gordon Ramsay an eight-figure sum.

"What's upsetting is that other people say racist things and yet I see their careers go very well – Ron Atkinson is on TV every week telling some manager how to run their team; others take bungs, which I always avoided, and succeed just as well. What did I do? I screamed at a bunch of what I felt were overpaid underachievers."

"What is the longest journey teams have had to make to play each other in any European competition?"

Cardiff City's Cup Winners' Cup campaign of 1967-68 appears to hold the answer. The quarter-final draw pitted the Bluebirds against Torpedo Moscow but, due to freezing conditions in Moscow, the away leg was staged in Tashkent (now the Uzbekistan capital), approximately 5,438km away. Cardiff lost the match 1-0, but a win in the first leg by the same margin forced a third play-off match at a neutral venue in Augsburg, West Germany, which they again won 1-0 thanks to Norman Dean's goal. Sadly, their European odyssey was ended in the semi-finals, where SV Hamburg beat them 4-3 on aggregate.

The 1994 Cup Winners' Cup clashes between Keflavík of Iceland and Israel's Maccabi Tel-Aviv are close behind at a distance of 5,269km. Eighty kilometres further back is the 2005 Champions League qualifier involving Azerbaijani representatives Neftci Baku and Icelandic outfit FJ (Hafnarfjördur).

"Can anyone tell me why the Spurs emblem is a chicken on a beach ball?"

Ken Ferris deals best with this query in his book, *Football: Terms and Teams*. "The club badge consists of a cockerel standing above a football marked with the initials THFC, flanked by a lion on each side, taken from the Northumberland family crest," wrote Ferris. "The badge is related to Harry Hotspur's riding spurs, since fighting cocks were once fitted out with miniature spurs. The full club crest clearly shows these. The cockerel and ball first appeared in 1909 when former player William James Scott cast a copper statue to perch on the new West Stand. The cockerel motif has been used on the shirts since the 1901 FA Cup final when Spurs became the first and so far only amateur team to win the trophy. The badge also includes, at the top left, a representation of Bruce Castle, the 16th-century building that now houses the local council's museum covering the history of Haringey. The museum is situated off Bruce Grove, around 400 yards from the ground. At the top right are seven trees planted at Page Green by the seven sisters of Tottenham after whom Seven Sisters Road and the Tube station are named."

"I was surprised to learn that former Tottenham goal machine Clive Allen had a brief spell as specialist goal-kicker with the NFL Europe outfit London Monarchs. Have any other footballers ever had any success in the sport?"

Few "soccer" players have been as successful in both sports as Toni Fritsch. Nicknamed "Wembley Toni" after scoring a memorable brace for Austria in a come-from-behind 3-2 win over Alf Ramsey's England at Wembley in 1965, diminutive forward Fritsch was spotted by then Dallas Cowboys coach Tom Landry on a scouting trip to Europe in 1971. According to Uefa, Landry offered Fritsch a contract after just one session kicking a pigskin through the posts. "I never saw a game before; I never saw a football," recalled Fritsch years later. "And I signed a contract with him [Landry] a couple days later, a contract that I couldn't read, but it was maybe the best contract I ever signed in my life and my career."

His American football career was certainly a successful one – spanning 12 seasons from 1971 to 1982, and including a Super Bowl win with Dallas in 1972 (he remains the only Austrian to ever win the Super Bowl) and a Pro Bowl (all-star game) appearance when he was with the Houston Oilers in 1980. Former Cowboys personnel director Gil Brandt remembered an incident in Fritsch's debut, when he kicked a winning field goal. "It was one of the funniest things I've ever seen," Brandt said.

"A linebacker for the [St Louis] Cardinals was hollering, 'Choke, Fritsch, choke!' and Dave Edwards, our upback on the protection team, said, 'He can't understand English.'" In all, Fritsch played for four NFL clubs, spending a year with each of the San Diego Chargers (1976) and New Orleans Saints (1982), on top of longer spells with the Cowboys (1971-75) and Oilers (1977-1981), scoring 758 points in 125 games. Afterwards he also played briefly for the Houston Gamblers in the USFL.

Fritsch wasn't the first European footballer to kick in the NFL, though. German Horst Muhlmann played for Schalke 04 from 1962-66 before resurfacing Stateside, aged 29, with the Cincinnati Bengals in 1969. He eventually played nine seasons in the NFL (Bengals 1969-74, Philadelphia Eagles 1975-77), and remains something of a celebrity in Cincinnati, where he owns two bars in the Bengals' Paul Brown Stadium. Shortly after Muhlmann retired, two American soccer-playing brothers – Chris and Matt Bahr – made a similar switch, giving up careers in another doomed league – the North American Soccer League (NASL) – to kick in the NFL. Sons of NASL Hall-of-famer Walter Bahr, Chris and Matt quit the Philadelphia Atoms and the Colorado Caribous in 1976 and 1979 respectively, going on to enjoy long and successful gridiron careers, both of which included Super Bowl wins.

Many more professional footballers have enjoyed lower-level gridiron spells – with the former Borussia

Dortmund and Werder Bremen striker Manfred Burgsmüller, and the Barcelona keeper Jesús Mariano Angoy among a number to have kicked in NFL Europe. Likewise, many successful NFL kickers showed promise as footballers without ever going professional; most notably Morten Andersen, who became the NFL's all-time leading scorer in 2007 with 2,445 points, after nearly making the Danish national junior side as a youngster.

"Upon reading your old article about football-inspired band names, I got to thinking about football-inspired albums, such as Half Man Half Biscuit's All I Want for Christmas is a Dukla Prague Away Kit. Do you know of any other songs or albums?"

The aforementioned Half Man Half Biscuit had a track, rather than an album called All I Want for Christmas Is a Dukla Prague Away Kit and it was released as the B-side on debut single The Trumpton Riots. A paean to Subbuteo and Scalextric, it contained the lyrics "and he'd managed to get hold of a Dukla Prague away kit "cause his uncle owned a sports shop and he'd kept it to one side".

Super Furry Animals wrote The Man Don't Give a Fuck about the Reading and Cardiff City legend Robin Friday – the single features Friday flicking a V-sign on its cover. "He was the superstar of the suburbs, the one who made George Best look like a lightweight," wrote Paolo Hewitt and former Oasis bassist Paul McGuigan in their book, *The Greatest Footballer You Never Saw: The Robin Friday Story*.

Chumbawamba included Song for Len Shackleton on their Readymades album, brothers Sebastien and Emmanuel Lipszyc penned Coupe de Boule as a tribute to Zinédine Zidane's 2006 World Cup final attack on Marco Materazzi, and Mogwai wrote the fantastic score to the movie Zidane: A 21st Century Portrait. Audiotransparent named their second album Nevland after the former FC Groningen and Fulham forward, while The Proclaimers' Sunshine on Leith is a somewhat soppy song written about their beloved Hibernian.

The Fall's Kicker Conspiracy, meanwhile, is possibly the most all-encompassing football song ever. It deals with players ("in the booze club George Best does rule"), the football authorities ("in the marble halls of the charm school/How flair is punished/Under marble Millichip the FA broods/On how flair can be punished"), the media ("J Hill's satanic reign") and hooliganism ("remember, you are abroad/Remember the police are rough").

"A friend told me that Ajax won the Dutch Cup in 1970 despite being knocked out in an earlier round. Surely not?"

Sure is. Ajax were beaten in the round of 16 by AZ Alkmaar, but there were actually only 15 teams left in the competition at that stage, so one of the seven losers got the gift of a quarter-final place. It was Ajax, and much to the KNVB's embarrassment they went on to win the cup after beating PSV 2-0 in the final. Ajax are not the only losers to win, of course. Nick Berry did with his seminal 1987 ballad, and Denmark won Euro 92 despite not actually qualifying for the tournament – they were included at the last minute when Yugoslavia were forced to pull out.

"In light of Real Madrid's sacking of Fabio Capello, are there any other managers who have been axed after winning the league title twice by the same club?"

Madrid actually only swung the axe at poor Fabio's head on one occasion; on the other, in 1997, he left the Bernabéu for Milan of his own accord. However, Vicente del Bosque *has* been effectively sacked by the club twice: first, during a short tenure as manager in 1994 and then, infamously, in 2003 when the club decided not to renew his contract even though he had just led the club to their second La Liga title in three seasons. He had also, somewhat shabbily, won two Champions League crowns in his four years in charge. "Del Bosque was showing signs of exhaustion," deadpanned the Madrid president Florentino Pérez, before somehow adding with a straight face: "I want to be sincere about this – our belief is that he was not the right coach for the future."

Even before Del Bosque, Madrid had form for severing the hand that feeds them: in 1998, they sacked German coach Jupp Heynckes after just one season – a season in which they won the European Cup for the first time in 32 years. Heynckes paid the price for some relatively miserable domestic form – Madrid finished fourth in La Liga, although they actually lost fewer games than the champions Barcelona – and was gone within eight days of the 1-0 victory over Juventus.

However, surely the hardest-done-by manager in history was the Bayern Munich boss Udo Lattek, also sacked by his paymasters on two occasions. "In 1975, after he had won three German championships in a row and the European Cup, a Bayern side full of tired World Cup winners only finished 10th in the league," recalled the Guardian's German football expert Raphael Honigstein. "Legend has it he then told club president Wilhelm Neudecker that 'things have to change', only to receive the reply: 'Yes, they have to: you're fired!' He was reappointed in 1983 and again won three German championships and two cups in four seasons. But the

European Cup final defeat in 1987 exposed a fraught relationship with his players. The club ultimately blamed him for the 2-1 loss against Porto and he was sacked. Again."

"Who have won the most cup competitions playing in their away kit?"

Without a doubt it is Milan, who have won six of seven European titles in their *maglia fortunata* (lucky jersey) since the team first triumphed against Benfica at Wembley in 1963. Even when they won the toss before the 2006 Champions League final, they chose to play in white instead of their trademark *rossoneri* red-and-black shirt (not that a white shirt did them many favours in 2005, mind). When they have played in red and black, Milan have won just one of three finals, beating Ajax in 1969. "Milan will play in white shirts," declared the club's vice-president Adriano Galliani prior to beating Liverpool. "Our first win was in [white] in '63 and we will go forward in that colour, for good or ill."

In an interview with the Times before Milan's win, London Medical Centre colour psychologist Ingrid Collins explained that "there are myths that people in white are something higher than human beings. We think of angels and knights in shining armour". Or Pippo Inzaghi actually beating an offside trap to score.

"I recently heard that Arsenal have an official club magician, whose job is to entertain corporate clients on match day. What other unusual non-football persons are employed by football clubs?"

Marvin Berglas began his association with Arsenal in 1993 when he became the Premier League's first ever resident magician. Son of the famous illusionist David Berglas, Marvin entertains VIPs and sponsors on match days and even plays in the Gunners' celebrity supporters team. "I am proud of my close association with Arsenal and of the magicians we provide on match days," he explains. Not wishing to be outdone by their old rivals, Spurs also have a magician entering his 10th consecutive season at White Hart Lane. Nicholas Einhorn, who was apparently a conjuring child prodigy, performs in the hospitality suites and private boxes prior to every home game. "What I enjoy is the moment of pure frozen amazement, the widening eyes and the puzzled lines across the brow," says Einhorn.

But it doesn't end there. On the other side of London, David Redfearn is an ever-present in all the corporate areas at Chelsea, and entertains guests at the club's Champions League matches. Meanwhile, Manchester United's card trick guru is Matt Windsor, who claims to be a first-class "magician and pickpocket". A winner of Sky One's TV talent quest – Next! – Matt has mixed humour and sleight of hand at Old Trafford for the last six seasons. Much like John O'Shea. As for other non-football employees hanging around at clubs, many do have the odd bizarre position or two going. Sarah Wardle is Spurs' poet in residence, Ian McMillan assumes the same role at Barnsley, while punk poet Attila the Stockbroker gains inspiration from Brighton and Hove Albion. Leicester City have an artist in residence, as do both Middlesbrough and Brentford.

"In the spirit of fair play, has any player in a top-level match intentionally missed a penalty given as the result of an egregiously bad ref decision?"

Amazingly they have, although contrary to popular opinion, Robbie Fowler is *not* one of them. While playing for Liverpool against Arsenal at Highbury on March 24 1997, Fowler was involved in a famous incident; he won a penalty, appearing to tumble under the challenge of David Seaman, before pleading with the referee Gerald Ashby not to award it, claiming the keeper had not touched him. Seaman saved the penalty, Jason McAteer rammed in the rebound, and Fowler ended up winning Uefa's Fair Play award for his honesty. However, Fowler admitted he did not miss on purpose. "As a goalscorer it's part of my job to take it and I wanted to score it," he claimed. "I tried to score. I never missed on purpose. It just happened, it was a bad penalty."

Unlike Fowler, the midfielder Morten Wieghorst did deliberately fire a spot kick wide while captaining Denmark against Iran at a Carlsberg Cup match in 2003. Thinking he had heard the referee whistle for half-time, an Iranian defender picked up the ball inside his penalty area; unfortunately the whistle had come from the stands. "It was unfair to capitalise on that," said Wieghorst, who subsequently consulted with his coach Morten Olsen before firing wide. Although Denmark subsequently lost 1-0, Wieghorst at least picked up an Olympic Committee fair play award.

Eduardo Galeano's brilliant work details an impressive example of sportsmanship during the Bogota derby between Millonarios and Club Santa Fe in 1967. The match had been heading for a draw when the Santa Fe striker Lorenzo Devanni tripped himself up in the area, and was promptly awarded a penalty. "No one had touched him," wrote Galeano. "He wanted to tell the referee it was a mistake, but the Santa Fe players picked him up and carried him on a stretcher to the white penalty spot. Between the posts, the hangman's posts, waited the keeper. He knew what he was going to do and the price he was going to pay. He chose ruin; he chose glory: Devanni took a running start and with all his might kicked it wide, far wide of the goal."

However, the one-time London giants Corinthians disagreed with the whole notion of penalties when they were originally introduced to the game. Adhering to their own club's code of conduct, Corinthians were adamant no side would intentionally cheat, and consequently missed any penalty they were given, while their keepers refused to save any given against them – trusting the opposition to decide whether they felt they had been wronged and score or miss accordingly. Come the turn of the 20th century, the code was amended.

"We all know about Escape to Victory and Goal, but which other films have included 'acting' roles for footballers?"

Despite having more than 30 credits to his name, Vinnie Jones fails to make the list because he doesn't act so much as play Vinnie Jones in every single turkey he appears in. Then again, Eric Cantona only ever plays an enigmatic Frenchman in his films, but he's appeared in the Oscar-winning Elizabeth – which stomps all over Garfield: A Tale of Two Kitties – so he gets the thumbs-up over Vinnie.

Elsewhere – as well being Match of the Day's host and the eponymous, brooding hero of kids' show Underground Ernie – Gary Lineker starred with his now ex-wife Michelle as "Couple in Restaurant" in the seminal 1993 comedy Splitting Heirs. Fellow striker Stan Collymore starred in the bongo-fest that was Basic Instinct 2 as Sharon Stone's boyfriend, although [spoiler alert] poor

Stan doesn't even survive the opening credits. "He is the loveliest, most chivalrous, most charming and most professional person," gushed Stone about her co-star afterwards. Then again, she claimed the tragic 2008 earthquake in China was "karma" for the government's treatment of Tibet.

Ally McCoist, Steve Tosh, Didier Agathe and Owen Coyle appeared alongside Hollywood heavy-hitters Robert Duvall, Brian Cox and Michael Keaton in A Shot at Glory. McCoist is the star striker in Duvall's plucky

Scottish side Kilnockie. And who can forget Archie Gemmill's appearance in Trainspotting? His goal from the 1978 World Cup is playing in the background during a scene that ultimately leads to Tommy's drug addiction and death. Still, it's a pretty good goal.

Chelsea's Nicolas Anelka appeared in the 2002 film Le Boulet playing the part of Nicolas, a footballer. In a thrilling if sadly rare Knowledge exclusive, Anelka explained that a career in the movies is all but guaranteed once he hangs up his boots. "I have a friend who's a producer, who makes lots of films," said the Frenchman. "He recently did Asterix. So it's already agreed that I'm going to do other films. It helps to know actors and producers. It's different to football and it's something I enjoy very much because there's no ball. I like pretending to be somebody else, it's fun."

Highbury features in 1939's The Arsenal Stadium Mystery, which was filmed at the Gunners' former home. The plot centres around a player who drops dead during an Arsenal home game, and several players and staff, including Cliff Bastin and manager George Allison, appear as themselves. Other clubs and their players starring in films include Newcastle United (Purely Belter) and Sheffield United (When Saturday Comes).

It's not just British-based footballers that have turned their hands to the dramatic arts, though. World Cup winner and former Bayern Munich midfielder Paul Breitner starred as Sergeant Stark in spaghetti western,

Potato Fritz. On a similarly continental tip, the Italian actor Raf Vallone, best known on these shores for roles in The Italian Job and The Godfather Part III, once played for Torino. And Andrew Shue, brother of Elizabeth, combined professions when turning out for LA Galaxy while starring in soap opera Melrose Place. The Shue siblings also teamed up to produce Gracie, a film loosely based on Elizabeth's experience of playing football in a boys' team when she was growing up.

But when it comes to unlikely hotbeds of acting talent, Oldham Athletic, circa 2002-03, has to be right up there. They boasted one player who appeared in a major Hollywood movie, and another who turned down the opportunity to do the same. Fitz Hall was the bona fide star, having appeared in The Fifth Element. "I try to keep it quiet but I'm there at the start," he said. "You can't miss me. I still get phone calls from people saying, 'Is that you in the film? There's a little kid looks just like you.' I was only 12 at the time but I've not changed." Meanwhile, Wayne Andrews, one of the footballers who appeared in the Vinnie vehicle Mean Machine, refused to appear alongside Angelina Jolie in Tomb Raider 2 after being offered terms by the Latics. "There isn't a steady income in acting, but football is different," he said. "The lads have nicknamed me Eddie Murphy."

"A litre bottle of a certain beer is known as a 'Drogba' in the Ivory Coast, on account of it being big and strong. Have any other footballers lent their name to certain foods or drink?"

The French fast-food chain Quick signed up Nicolas Anelka in 2007 to release the peppery "Anelka Burger", while there are also the more obvious Walkers crisps examples of "Salt and [Gary] Lineker" and "Cheese and [Michael] Owen" (sadly for fans of comedy defending, "Titus [Bramble]" Sweet Chilli Sensations are yet to hit the production line). However, when it comes to booze, there are several rather more obscure cases.

Take the Andy Porter, brewed briefly in 1996 by the Titanic Brewery in Burslem, Stoke-on-Trent, in honour of the eponymous Port Vale midfielder who made 357 appearances for the club between 1987 and 1998. By the time he retired in 2006, the Andy Porter was no more. When the Knowledge called Titanic to find out what happened to this 5% ale, we were told "it was a one-off for one person". Andy Porter, presumably. Mart Poom might just be the only goalkeeper to have a beer named after him, though. Poominator Ale is thought to derive from a piece of commentary by Simon Crabtree on Metro Radio in the north-east after Poom equalised in the last minute of Sunderland's Championship game against Derby at Pride Park in September 2003. The words, "It's the Poominator. He'll be back," appear to have inspired one listener to brew the aforementioned ale. "I don't drink beer," said Poom later, "but it was a nice gesture and meant I had some presents for my friends."

And according to the Campaign for Real Ale's website (Wigan branch), the Chimblonda, named in honour of erstwhile Latics defender Pascal Chimbonda, also had a brief lifespan several years ago. It cost £2 a pint, clocked in at 4.3%, and was a "new beer from Wigan's brewery, brewed specially for the festival. A very pale beer using Challenger and Cascade hops."

"Who were the first team to score 1,000 goals in the Premier League, and which team was the first to score 1,000 goals in the old First Division?"

We're pretty sure every reader over the age of four will remember Manchester United becoming the first team to score 1,000 in the Rupert Murdoch League, Cristiano Ronaldo scoring the 1,000th against Middlesbrough on October 29 2005. Not so many of you will recall Aston Villa becoming the first team to score 1,000 league goals back in 1904.

No one, however, has managed the feat achieved by Bury, who remain the only team to have scored 1,000 goals at every level of League football. Bury sealed their place in history on August 27 2005, when Brian Barry-Murphy scored their first equaliser in a 2-2 draw with

Wrexham in League Two. Previously, they had reached a top-flight thousand with a Norman Bullock goal against Sheffield United in December 1926, matched that achievement in the old Division Two when Eddie Gleadall struck against Huddersfield in March 1953 and again in the third tier with David Lee's finish in May 1997 against Blackpool.

"Other than Blackburn's David 'Betnley' gaffe in 2007, have there been any other instances of footballers' names being spelt wrongly on the back of their shirts?"

Let's begin with one of the more well-known mistakes, the time David Beckham morphed into David "Beckam" during the 1997 Charity Shield against Chelsea. "I thought the lads were winding me up," Beckham said at the time. "Then I saw it for myself. It was too late to do anything about it, so we all had a laugh instead." If you think such basic typographical errors are limited to one of the richest sporting institutions in the world, you'd be half right. When John O'Shea turned out for Manchester United against Real Madrid in the Champions League quarter-final second leg at Old Trafford in April 2003, his shirt bore the legend 'S'hea'.

And it gets no better. Ole Gunnar Solskjaer's name was spelt "Solksjaer" when they played Newcastle in

2002-03, while their Polish goalkeeper Tomasz Kuszczak completes a less than fab four. Now, the potential pitfalls here demand sympathy; except that the person responsible for imprinting names on shirts was presumably concentrating so hard on that tricky "zcz" combo that when Kuszczak played only his second game for United, in a Carling Cup tie against Crewe in October 2006, he mysteriously became "Zuszczak".

Newcastle "defender" Jean-Alain Boumsong turned out as "Boumsogn" against Liverpool in March 2005, but at least that howler wasn't as poorly timed and embarrassing as Sunderland's back in 2001, when they set Don "Hucthison" up for a ribbing in the Tyne and Wear derby. The Guardian's very own Steve Claridge also confirmed that he shrugged off the indignity of becoming "Clarridge" during a televised game for Leicester against Sheffield Wednesday in 1996-97 to score, while Costa Rica's Mauricio Wright was turned into "Wrigth" for a World Cup game against China in 2002.

As for the best howler-related chant? "There's only one H in Palace," as sung by the Selhurst Park faithful after the club's name was rendered 'Chrystal' on the team shirt's badge in 2004.

"Who is the youngest player to reach 100 international caps?"

The honour, in actual fact, currently belongs to US women's striker Cindy Parlow who, at 23 years, one month and 26 days, brought up her century while captaining the American side in a friendly against Canada. So impressive was the team's performance under her leadership that day, it caused coach April Heinrichs to claim: "My emotions and arousal level were as high today as they were for any game in the Olympics." At the time of writing, Parlow is also the youngest person to have won both an Olympic gold medal and the women's World Cup.

"Is the Euro 2008 group of Holland, Italy, France and Romania the deadliest group ever at a European Championship or World Cup?"

The average Fifa ranking of the teams in Group C is 8, but this is not the most statistically perilous collection of hopefuls to have been thrown together since the ranking system began in December 1992. The "deadliest" group of death, by some way, belongs to Group C in the 1996 European Championship. While England dealt with Holland and Scotland, eventual victors Germany (at the time ranked No2 in the world) were lumped in with

Russia (3), Italy (7), and the Czech Republic (10), giving a bone-chilling average of 5.5. France were also forced to negotiate a hazardous passage through the group stage on the way to winning Euro 2000. Although the average team ranking was 9.75, this was skewed by Holland being positioned at 21 when the tournament began, despite going on to top the group.

Before the rankings came into existence, however, the title surely must go to Argentina, Brazil and Italy being drawn together in the second group stage of the 1982 World Cup, with only one to qualify. Unsurprisingly, this system was only used once.

"In Roy Hattersley's book, *The Edwardians*, there's a photo described as 'the Edwardian England football team'. They are wearing white shirts and dark shorts, but curiously the shirts bear the union flag rather than the flag of St George. Was the union flag generally used by England teams back then, or was it just a cock-up?"

The union flag was the favoured emblem of English football teams until surprisingly recently. Footage of the 1966 World Cup shows Wembley dotted with red, white and blue flags, while tournament mascot World Cup Willie was a lion wearing a union flag jersey. In 1982 Ron Greenwood's England squad were still urging us to "hear the roar of the red, white and blue" on official tune This Time, a seven-inch single with a union flag on the label. It was only really at Euro 96 that the nation's red-and-white fetish kicked in properly. Matthew Engel, writing in the Guardian, noted "this new cult of St George" after England's exit in the semi-finals. Ten years later 27% of English adults bought a flag of St George during the 2006 World Cup. And a fat lot of good it did too.

"Why do Israeli clubs – and the national team – play in European competitions? Surely they should be knocking about with Asian teams – their neighbours Syria, Jordan and Lebanon do."

You might have noticed Israel hasn't really got the best of relations with other countries in the Middle East. Don't take it from us though – here's Uefa's statement on the matter: "According to the Uefa statutes, in exceptional circumstances, a national football association that is situated in another continent may be admitted for membership, provided that it is not a member of the confederation of that continent, or of any other confederation, and that Fifa approves its membership of Uefa. Due to the tense political situation in this particular part of the world in the beginning of the 1990s, Israel asked for its affiliation to Uefa. Its clubs were not given the chance to participate in club competitions under the umbrella of the Asian Football Confederation as most of the Arab countries objected to meeting Israeli teams.

"In an effort to contribute to the development of football and to give an opportunity to as many people as possible to enjoy the game, the Uefa executive committee decided to accept the affiliation request. This was done in three steps: September 19 1991 in Montreux, Switzerland: admission of teams from Israel in European clubs competitions; September 19 1993 in Cyprus: the Uefa executive committee agrees on a provisory admission of the Football Association of Israel (IFA); April 28 1994 in Vienna, Austria: the Uefa Congress agrees on a definite admission of the IFA to Uefa."

"I've just been Wiki-surfing and read on Peter Beardsley's page that he once scored four goals for England against Aylesbury United. Can anyone shed any light on when this game was played, why it was played, and if there have been any other similar friendlies?"

Picture the scene: it's eight days before Bobby Robson's England are due to run out at the Neckarstadion in Stuttgart for their opening match of the 1988 European Championships. You haven't lost an international since September 1987 and things are looking good. So who have you chosen for your final warm-up game? Aylesbury United? On June 4 1988 England completed their Euro 88 preparations against the reigning Beazer Homes (Southern) League champions in front of 6,031 at Buckingham Road. Beardsley did indeed net four goals in England's 7-0 thrashing of the Ducks, not that it did much good; England lost to Ray Houghton's goal against the Irish. Then lost to Holland. Then lost to the USSR. And then came home.

Aylesbury United remain the only non-league side to face the national team, but there have been other similar friendlies. On June 9 1998 England played a Caen XI in a behind-closed-doors game prior to the World Cup, with Paul Scholes scoring in a 1-0 win. Bradford City were beaten 2-1 by an England side in December 1986 in a match to celebrate the reopening of Valley Parade following the tragic fire in May 1985. And an FA XI – effectively the England team of the day – faced Bill Nicholson's double-winning Tottenham Hotspur side in the Charity Shield in August 1961. Spurs won 3-2.

"I vaguely remember a group of British players using a loophole to play for the Cayman Islands in the late 90s – Wayne Allison being among them. Did this actually happen, and if so was it a success (I assume not)?"

Such a loophole has sadly never been open, though that didn't stop the Cayman Islands from calling up eight British players anyway in late February 2000. The Caymans, as a British dependent territory, believed Fifa rules would allow them to call up players with a British passport, so long as they hadn't already been capped for another country. They employed agent Barry McIntosh to recruit the Brits ahead of their World Cup 2002 qualifier against Cuba, and he, expecting most players to turn him down, made formal approaches to 24 players. Surprisingly, 22 responded positively (though the highest profile – David May – did not), and in the end the Caymans were forced to let 14 of them down, settling on a quota of eight imports: the Tranmere captain Wayne Allison, Motherwell's Ged Brannan, Lincoln City's David Barnett, Birmingham's Martin O'Connor, Bristol City's Dwayne Plummer, Fulham's Barry Hayles, Southend United's Neville Roach and Boreham Wood's Neil Sharpe.

In the week before the first leg of their match against Cuba, all but Allison – who flew out later than the rest as he was needed for Tranmere's league game against

Portsmouth – represented the Caymans in a friendly against US champions DC United, and were duly thrashed 5-0. At this point, however, Fifa intervened, ruling that such players were not actually allowed to represent the Caymans unless they were Cayman-born nationals, five-year residents in the territory, or at least had links to the country through marriage or descendency. All but Sharpe and Barnett, who hung around to watch the tie anyway, returned to Britain before the first leg in Havana. The Caymans lost that game 4-0, and subsequently crashed out after only managing a goalless draw in the return.

"Are there any instances of companies losing money/sales/etc through their association with certain clubs?"

Everybody knows fans who proudly claim to avoid the products and services whose names adorn their rivals' shirts and stadia but, despite these boasts, evidence of companies actually losing money is scarce. There is, however, a unique situation with the Old Firm teams in Glasgow, who currently share the same sponsor: Carling. This began in 1984, when a small glazing company called CR Smith decided to sponsor both teams, and did so with massive success. Three years later, however, Rangers switched to McEwan's, causing large sections of

Celtic's support to stop drinking the beer – and several Celtic pubs to stop stocking it. The clubs eventually responded in 1999 by returning to shared sponsorship with NTL, and they have continued to stick with this system since.

In Italy, meanwhile, a short-lived "war of the cappuccino" broke out in Rome after Lazio bought Christian Vieri from Atlético Madrid in 1998. At the time, Lazio's president Sergio Cragnotti ran a food conglomerate called Cirio, which happened to raise its milk prices by about 3p per litre shortly after Vieri's arrival. Roma fans linked the two events – and were furious at what they perceived as being charged to fund Lazio's purchase. They responded by boycotting cappuccino, thereby reducing milk sales in the Italian capital.

More recently, a significant number of Manchester United fans rejected a number of brands for their continued association with the team after Malcolm Glazer's takeover. Vodafone did subsequently break their ties with the club, despite having time left to run on an existing contract, but their official reasoning for this was so that they could focus on Champions League sponsorship. Mars, meanwhile, scored a bit of an own goal in 2006 with their "Believe" campaign, which effectively supported England's bid to win the World Cup. "Even though Believe was confined to England, the global playground conspired to enable semi-organised boycotts of the product in Scotland, Wales and, bizarrely, Spain," wrote Dr Paul Springer in the book Ads to Icons. "Unfortunately, after another meek exit, even the English were left to grumble, 'They're not as big as they used to be.'"

"With the promotion of Accrington Stanley to the Football League, I got to wondering how they got the 'Stanley' suffix. What are the explanations behind other suffixes, like Crewe Alexandra, Plymouth Argyle, Preston North End and Tottenham Hotspur?"

According to the club's official website, "The original town team, Accrington FC, were amongst the 12 founder members of the Football League in 1888 before they resigned from the league after just five years. A team already existed at that time called Stanley Villa, named as such because they were based at the Stanley Arms on Stanley Street in the town. With the demise of Accrington FC, Stanley Villa took the town name."

David McKie's 2006 Guardian article acknowledged that "several of the less explicable names were originally invented for cricket. Sheffield Wednesday emerged from a cricket club that played its games on Wednesdays. Hotspur, as in Tottenham Hotspur, was chosen by a group of young men who had read about Harry Hotspur in Shakespeare's plays and thought it would be just the right dashing image for their new cricket club; the football developed later, as a sideline." While there is supposed debate as to the origins of Crewe's suffix, the club website appears to settle any disputes by stating that in "1877 – a football club is formed in Crewe, as a separate organisation from the successful Crewe Cricket Club. They take the name 'Alexandra' after Princess Alexandra." Preston, at least according to their website, were so named "simply as an indication of the club's base being in the north end of the town".

Last but not least, Plymouth's official website describes how "F Howard Grose and W Pethybridge shared rooms in the newly built Argyll Terrace (sometimes known as Argyle Terrace) while working in Plymouth. The two men wanted to pursue their interest in football and it was suggested it might be possible to form a new club by inviting old boys from local public schools to form a team. During a discussion on the name, Grose suggested the aim of the club should be to emulate the style of play used by the Argyll and Sutherland Highlanders, whose teamwork in winning the Army Cup had greatly impressed him. So the name Plymouth Argyle was born – and Argyle's first strip of green and black quarters is reminiscent of the S&A's tartan of large green and navy check overlaid with a few thin lines of white."

"Has a journalist ever represented his/her nation in an international match?"

They have, albeit predominantly in Norway for one reason or another. Perhaps the most famous journalist/footballer in his home country is Jørgen Juve, who is still Norway's top scorer to this day. Juve made his international debut against Finland in 1928 and was also hired as the sports editor of Dagbladet at the same time. More remarkable still is that he achieved his goal record of 33 in 45 starts despite starting more than half those matches as a defender.

Goalkeeper Ola by Rise enjoyed a lengthy footballing career from 1977 to 1995, in which time he combined shot-stopping at Rosenborg with filing copy for Trondheim newspaper Adresseavisen. By Rise spent most of his international career as understudy to Erik Thorstvedt; despite playing for Norway on 25 occasions, his 54 other appearances on the Norway bench earned him the unenviable record of international football's least-used substitute.

"Who is the most prolific goalscorer from corners in history?"

The Worthing midfielder Mark Pulling scored a hat-trick of corners in a 3-1 Ryman League (South) win at Corinthian Casuals in 2004, which stands out in terms of a one-game haul. But in terms of career statistics, it still falls a good way short. "Blackburn winger Morten Gamst Pedersen once scored six goals directly from a corner in the same match," explained Dag Langerød from the sports section of online Norwegian newspaper Nettavisen. "I interviewed him about this a couple of years ago. 'I think I was into my last year as a junior player when I scored six goals directly from a corner against local team Alta,' he told me. 'I scored four with my left and two with my right foot – all into the opposite top corner.'"

Mustafa Denizli, the former Turkish international, was suggested as a potential record holder with as many as 18 corner goals, but in following up this lead, we stumbled upon the name of another legendary Turkish player, Sükrü Gülesin. "Between 1940 and 1954 he played for Beyogluspor, Besiktas, Palermo, Lazio and Galatasaray," said Özgür Canbas, a presenter on Radyo Spor. "During his career he scored 226 goals; of these, 32 came directly from corners. In the 1950s this apparently appeared in the *Guinness Book of Records* as a world best. His major characteristic was that he could score these both from the left and right sides – even though he was left-footed."

"My late Dad used to tell a tale of a footballer he met on the train once, who scored nine times for his side and still lost 10-9! Is this true?"

We couldn't find any evidence of the aforementioned match, nor any performance to match the suggested nine-goal haul. However, there are still plenty of examples of players' heroic efforts going unrewarded thanks to their shambling accomplices.

Take Dariusz Dziekanowski, for example, who scored four times in a 1989 Uefa Cup clash with Partizan Belgrade, only for the Celtic backline to concede four at the other end. Trailing 5-3 in the last minute, Partizan launched one final attack, making the score 5-4 and claiming the tie on away goals. Kerry Dixon also scored four for Reading in a 1982-83 Third Division game at Doncaster – not that it counted for much: the Royals went down 7-5.

But surely the hardest-done-by player must be poor old Denis Law. Playing for Manchester City in an FA Cup fourth-round tie at Luton in 1961, Law scored six times as City raced into a 6-2 lead, only for the match to be abandoned. The Kenilworth Road pitch "first resembled a beach with the tide just out, then [there was] deep mud, then a shallow lake", according to one report of the game. "It's not every day that you score six goals," recalled Law in 2007. "I never did it again – the most I managed in a game that counted was four, which

I got a couple of times. But then the heavens opened. Obviously it wasn't meant to be. The funny thing was when we went for the replay on the Wednesday the pitch was in a worse state than it ever was on Saturday." As the law of Sod dictates, Law still scored in the second match, only for City to slump to a 3-1 defeat.

"When was the last time the England starting line-up contained no players from Manchester United?"

The team that faced Belgium on October 10 1999 at Sunderland's Stadium of Light comprised: David Seaman (Arsenal); Martin Keown (Arsenal), Tony Adams (Arsenal), Gareth Southgate (Aston Villa); Kieron Dyer (Newcastle), Paul Ince (Middlesbrough), Jamie Redknapp (Liverpool), Frank Lampard (West Ham), Steve Guppy (Leicester City); Alan Shearer (Newcastle), Kevin Phillips (Sunderland). More significant, perhaps, was the last time England began a competitive match without a United player. The answer? That fateful night of June 26 1996, when they lost to Germany in the Euro 96 semi-final. Gary Neville was suspended, David Beckham was six weeks away from changing his life from the halfway line at Selhurst Park, Paul Scholes was a supersub, Teddy Sheringham was a Spurs player, and Phil Neville was sitting with his brother on the England bench. The starting XI that night – as you all should know, of course – was: Seaman (Arsenal); Adams (Arsenal), Southgate (Aston Villa), Stuart Pearce (Nottingham Forest); Steve McManaman (Liverpool), David Platt (Arsenal), Ince (Internazionale), Paul Gascoigne (Rangers), Darren Anderton (Tottenham); Teddy Sheringham (Tottenham), Shearer (Newcastle).

"Going back a bit, is it true that AC Milan were in fact scouting John Barnes but signed Luther Blissett by mistake?"

Unsurprisingly, no one has ever admitted to committing such a ludicrous error but the tale is still alive and well in Italy, where there is even a prominent anarchist society named after the man who was sensationally lured from Watford to Serie A for £1m in July 1983, only to return to Vicarage Road a year later after flopping spectacularly. In a bid to get to the bottom of the matter, we sought the views of Italian football journalist Gabriele Marcotti. "There are two main reasons for which I think it's not true," he said. "First, even the most ignorant and provincial person could see that Blissett and Barnes looked absolutely nothing alike. Second, the fact is that at that time Milan were looking for an out-and-out goalscorer and Barnes just wasn't that type of player."

But what of Luther Blissett, the group of Italian activists? "In 1994, hundreds of European artists, activists and pranksters adopted and shared the same identity," explains *www.lutherblissett.net*. "They all called themselves Luther Blissett and set to raising hell in the cultural industry. It was a five-year plan. They worked together to tell the world a great story, create a legend, give birth to a new kind of folk hero. In January 2000, some of them regrouped as Wu Ming. The latter project, albeit more focused on literature and storytelling in the narrowest sense of the word, is no less radical than the old one." The group's book *Q* even made it on to the longlist for the Guardian's First Book Award in 2003.

"Has a footballer ever been arrested on the field of play?"

In 2005, police swooped on the Quilmes defender Leandro Desábato at the final whistle of his team's 3-1 Copa Libertadores defeat to São Paulo. Desábato, it was alleged, had racially slandered opposition striker Grafite and was summarily hauled off to a local police station for questioning. "There's no need for all this chaos," complained the Quilmes coach Gustavo Alfaro after the game. "A football match should start and finish on the pitch. This has all been handled in the wrong way. It was an unnecessary spectacle [for the police] to come on to the field in front of 50,000 or 60,000 people when the player's pulse-rate is still high. He's just lost a game." Desábato was released on £2,000 bail after spending a night in the cells, but no charges were ever brought against him.

The Botafogo defender Andre Luis was also dragged off the field by riot police during a Brazilian championship match at Nautico in June 2008. Luis, sent off for a second booking, reacted furiously to the decision, antagonising opposition fans and sparking a free-for-all among the players. Officers eventually arrested the defender, but not before pepper-spraying his brawling team-mates and opponents. "Footballers are not bandits, and are not to be kicked and punched. This has to stop," raged the Botafogo president Bebeto de Freitas, who was also arrested. "The player was wrong, he will be punished and suspended. What is not acceptable is for him to have pepper in his face or be prodded in the back with a truncheon." Both Luis and De Freitas were released after questioning.

Back in England, the Droylsden FC forward Paddi Wilson also felt the long arm of the law while he was warming up ahead of an FA Trophy tie against Ashton in 2002. Greater Manchester police arrived on the scene and Wilson was accompanied to the changing rooms for questioning, before being taken to the local nick. "Patrick Wilson was arrested on failing to appear in court in connection with outstanding road traffic offences," confirmed a spokesman for the force. Droylsden went on to win the game 2-1.

"Much like Neil Webb, former Dutch international Berry van Aerle is apparently a postman now. What is the strangest job a retired footballer has taken up?"

Joining a surprisingly lengthy list of ex-player posties are Kevin Hector (Derby), the former Leeds and Scotland goalkeeper David Harvey (in the Orkney Islands, where he's also a farmer), and even Peter Bonetti, who had a spell delivering joy to the residents of the Isle of Mull. But we're after more random post-career occupations, and another former Tottenham player, John Chiedozie, definitely fits the bill as . . . a bouncy castle vendor. He currently runs his own company, renting out inflatables and animals for children's parties in Hampshire. Another ex-Spur, Peter Collins, became a market trader in Romford, while Gudni Bergsson went on to practise law in his native Iceland.

Even 1966 World Cup winner and Everton full-back Ray Wilson had to broaden his vocational horizons, becoming an undertaker in Huddersfield after ending his career. Then there is Alan Comfort, formerly of Leyton Orient and Middlesbrough, who is now a vicar –

and chaplain for the Os. Also setting up shop was one-time Dundee United midfield enforcer Davy Bowman, who maintained his hardman reputation . . . by running a Tayside flower shop with his wife.

But for sheer inventiveness, our favourite post-football career is that of Tomas Brolin. According to the Premier League website's own comprehensive "Where are they now?" section, "After leaving football, Brolin returned to Sweden and involved himself in a number of business ventures, including selling shoes and vacuum cleaners on the internet, before taking part-ownership of a property firm with his father and establishing a restaurant in Stockholm. He also made a record with Doctor Alban, starred in a Jacuzzi advert, and hit the headlines after his car collided with an elk."

Acknowledgments

The list of contributors and colleagues who have given their time and help to the column over the years is a long one and apologies go to anyone who has been unfairly omitted. Should there ever be another book in this series, we'll be sure to have an 'Acknowledgments (2)' section. Nevertheless, the hard work and football brains of Sean Ingle and Scott Murray deserve particular thanks, along with Rob Smyth, Georgina Turner, Paul Doyle, John Ashdown, Paolo Bandini, Tom Lutz, Sid Lowe, Raphael Honigstein and Jonathan Wilson, among many others. The dedicated team at Guardian Books, too, must be credited with transforming our ideas into a published reality. Last, but very much not least, Knowledge readers warrant our immense gratitude. Without their correspondence, the tone and content of the column would not be what it is today.